Forget it...
What's the Point?

Also by Marguerite Orane:
Free and Laughing: Spiritual Insights in EveryDay Moments

Forget It!
What's the Point?

Letting Go and Claiming Joy

MARGUERITE ORANE

First published in Canada 2018 by
Free and Laughing Inc.
2911 Bayview Avenue
Toronto, ON M2K1E8,
Canada
www.margueriteorane.com
E-mail: marguerite@margueriteorane.com

© 2018 by Marguerite Orane

All rights reserved. This book may not be reproduced in whole or in part without permission from the author, except by a reviewer who may quote brief passages in a review; nor may any part of this book be reproduced, stored in a retrieval system, or transmitted in any form or by any means, electronic, mechanical, photocopying, recording, or other, without written permission from the author.

ISBN: 978-1-9994078-0-3 (print)
978-1-9994078-1-0 (ebook)

A catalogue record of this book is available
from the Library and Archives Canada.

Cover and book design by Robert Harris
(email: roberth@cwjamaica.com)
Set in Centaur 13.5/19 x 21
Printed in the United States of America

*For my siblings,
Douglas and Carole,
who demonstrate daily that love is boundless, accepting,
generous and unconditional;
and my children,
Marc, Victoria and Shane —
you are my greatest teachers and joy*

CONTENTS

Foreword *ix*
Archbishop Emeritus Desmond Mpilo Tutu

Preface *ix*

1. A Beautiful Dying *1*
2. I Keep Losing Diamond Earrings *12*
3. The Maiden Aunt *19*
4. No-One Wants the Bottom Bunk *24*
5. My Father's Boss *28*
6. A Chance Encounter with a Pipe *37*
7. Crowning Glory *43*
8. The Artist *51*
9. Butterfly Wings *60*
10. Laughing at the Dirty Dishes *66*
11. Happiness Backlash *70*
12. Smashed and Imperfect Things *76*
13. You Deserve a Name *81*

CONTENTS

14   From Home   *88*

15   The Day Can Wait   *97*

16   Miss Chin Picks Up the Poop   *102*

17   To Home   *106*

18   From Bay Street to Bayview   *113*

19   A Cloud of Love   *119*

20   After the Ecstasy, the Toilet   *128*

21   Bug Meditation   *132*

        Where Mi Navel String Bury –
        My Jamaican Foundation   *139*

        In Gratitude   *149*

        About The Author   *153*

FOREWORD

Our stories are important and powerful in our own healing and in helping others to heal.

My work on the Truth and Reconciliation Commission in South Africa opened the space for those who had been deeply affected by apartheid to safely share their stories, release the suffering, forgive, heal and hopefully, move on with their lives. In this way, we started the process of healing our nation and the world.

In *Forget It! What's the Point?* Marguerite Orane shares her stories at various junctures in her life. There are small things – trying to get her children to do the dishes, losing family heirloom diamond earrings, a neighbour who didn't clean up after her dog, her morning routine. And some big ones – her mother's transition, her experience with her father when she ran her family's business, leaving Jamaica, moving to Canada and her challenge in finding a job, despite an MBA from Harvard. There are stories about relationships – her beloved aunt, a neighbour, a chance meeting in Rio with a very interesting gentleman.

FOREWORD

And there's even a piece from one of her beloved dogs, who really seems to get the point. These stories reveal Marguerite delving deeply, telling her truth and going through the process of releasing and renewing herself. It is very similar to the Fourfold Forgiveness Process that we developed during the Truth and Reconciliation Commission.

In one of the chapters in this book, Marguerite writes: "I once met Archbishop Desmond Tutu. He laughed the whole time. No, he didn't do laughter, he was laughter itself, happiness and joy in his very being — his default state. I think about his life under apartheid in South Africa, how terrible it must have been. I think of his best friend, the Dalai Lama, who lives in exile, his life always under threat, unable to return to Tibet, his beloved home country. Yet, two happier men you would never see. I keep their "Book of Joy" beside my bed, their smiling faces one of the first things I see in the morning."

I am humbled to see the impact I have had on this one life, and to see her continue the work of healing the world by sharing her own healing, thus helping others to forgive and find lasting happiness and joy.

Archbishop Emeritus Desmond Mpilo Tutu
Hermanus, South Africa
July, 2018

PREFACE

On May 12, 2008, my mother died: four and a half months after her 90th birthday, the day after Mother's Day and six weeks after taking to her bed for the journey of leaving her body. During those six weeks, she often made this statement, disguised as a question, that puzzled us, her loved ones:

"Forget it. What's the point?"

I migrated to Canada from Jamaica the year after my mother passed. I sold most of my possessions and closed my business, intending to be unencumbered and free, open to the possibilities of a new country. But there were things that I was holding on to — relationships, material treasures, opinions, beliefs, people, minor incidents in my life. "Let go, let go, let go", didn't seem to work. More, and more, I recalled Mummy's parting words. And I started to ask of each "it" that I faced, or had faced: "What's the point?"

PREFACE

The search for my corner, my nest, my identity in this new place led me to the University of Toronto School of Continuing Studies where I met Lee Gowan, the director of the Creative Writing Program: "You must come to our Summer Creative Writing Intensive," he told me when I presented him with a copy of my book, *Free and Laughing: Spiritual Insights in Every Day Moments*, and shared that I journaled, hosted a blog and was interested in learning about writing. I chuckled as I realised how often in my life I had done things backways – write a book, then learn to write! I shelved the idea in my "one day I shall" folder. Then, two years later, an ad for the Summer Intensive popped up on my Facebook page. I registered for "Meditation and Writing" and had the greatest fun at what I call a "summer camp for adults". Coming from the corporate world where we are admonished to be brief, to the point, impersonal and without emotion, I struggled with character development, plot, dialogue and other creative writing techniques. I started to dig deep into some of those "it" things. Writing forces you to do that. I discovered that I could apply the gifts of memory and imagination to

PREFACE

my personal experiences, so that my writing became cathartic, but also expansive. I could build on some minor incident and create a riveting story that was not quite the actuality of what happened, but which became my truth.

In the Fall after the Summer Intensive, I signed up for another course, then another, until I found I had completed the requirements to prepare for the final project for the Certificate in Creative Writing. But what could I write to satisfy the 20,000 word minimum requirement? By now I had started my own business and was travelling to the Caribbean every month. I had no time to write 20,000 words from scratch! I consulted Ranjini George, one of my Creative Writing professors, who had become my mentor, and I daresay, a friend. As we sat one afternoon in our favourite café on Bloor Street, she pointed out that I had already done the writing:

"I love that one about your mother's transitioning, Marguerite. It is so tender. Start the collection with that one. And how about the one about your dog? And that one about losing your diamond earrings? Look at all the pieces you have written for your other courses. Go back into your blogs. It's all there."

PREFACE

It was all there — on my computer, in my journals, in my mind, an endless river of creativity unleashed by the program. This book is the result of my Certificate in Creative Writing Final Project. The moment I committed to it, I knew the title and the theme would be "Forget It! What's the Point? I consider it another gift from my mother, who inspired and gave me the title for my first book *Free and Laughing: Spiritual Insights in Every Day Moments.* It is a collection of some, a very few, of the mileposts over the course of my life that have presented great learning for me. I haven't forgotten these experiences, clearly, but in asking "What's the point?", they have become clouds in the sky of my mind — fleeting, without substance, changing form, fading away. With this release has come freedom and joy. Where memory failed — names, exact words of a conversation, dates — my imagination took charge. I changed some names for privacy, created dialogue and played with time. You will find throughout this book, proverbs and sayings from Jamaica, the land of my birth, where my navel string is buried (a traditional custom of burying a baby's umbilical

PREFACE

cord shortly after birth). There's a chapter at the end of the book in which I share the translation of each proverb and why I chose it. Wherever I go, Jamaica is part of me. That I do not forget.

I hope that you will enjoy my stories – laugh, perhaps shed a tear, or just wonder about my life. But perhaps you will also reflect on the "its" you have faced and are still holding on to, and ask yourself: "What's the point?"

Marguerite Orane

1

A BEAUTIFUL DYING

Fi mi love have lion heart
Strong and everlasting, only fi yuh.

My mother took six weeks to die. And it was beautiful.

I remember the moment I became aware that Mummy was dying. It was a Saturday morning, some three months after her 90th birthday and I was heading to the greengrocer to buy fruits and vegetables for the coming week. I called, as I did each week, to find out if she needed anything. She loved fresh fruit – papaya, mangoes, banana, grapefruit, pineapple and sweetsop, her favourite. I don't remember exactly what she said, because her words were like scattered jigsaw pieces. Marva, one of her caregivers, took the phone.

"Marva. What's wrong with Mummy?"

"Is so she going on all morning, Miss Marguerite. Not making any sense at all." And that was my first inkling that Mummy had begun her transition.

"What did your mother die from?" I was asked on numerous occasions in the months following her death, as if knowing made a difference.

"Well . . . nothing really," I would respond with a soft chuckle. "Her spirit just outgrew her body."

I have many examples, in hindsight, of people who transited and left clear messages and indications that they were preparing to go. Elsa, a dear friend of my mother, had a massive heart attack and died on the operating table while being prepped for her scheduled surgery. A week before, she had given away all her clothes. Bobby, my cousin's husband, with whom she owned a business, said to her one Sunday: "Let me show you everything about how to run this business." Two weeks later, he was killed in a freak accident. And my mother, who responded to my daughter Victoria's question:

"Are you spending Christmas with us next year,

Grandma?" with a shrugged, "I don't know about that." I think she did know, because she passed on in May of the following year.

In those six weeks, my mind raced with questions, pondering the presence of death snuggled in a bed in the form of my mother: Why are we so afraid of dying? Or is it that we are afraid of death? Or both? Yet, isn't death inevitable and certain to happen to us all? The only uncertainty is when and how, I mused. Do we get to choose? Is death as unconscious as we think it is? Is death something that is done to us? Is it a terrible event, despite the salvation promised by religion, to which we cling, hoping eternity exists? Do we each consciously or unconsciously decide when and how we will die? If death is something inevitable and something over which we might have control, how can the dying be?

Mummy took to her bed, and other than a week in hospital, remained there. Her family was witness to a process over the next six weeks of her releasing, wandering, returning and then finally departing. There were moments of sadness, frustration, laughter, joy and most of all, love. Some days she lay in the twin bed lodged against the wall in her bedroom, eyes glazed and fixed, through the wooden-louvred window, far beyond and above the Jamaican Blue Mountains that hug the city of Kingston. We, her children, grandchildren, friends and caregivers, perched on the other twin bed, or hovering at her feet, would watch and wonder . . . Where was she? Sometimes she would roll her eyes, purse her lips and emit a deep sigh. And then return. Once my sister, Carole, asked her where she had been. "I can't tell you that," she said, with a wisp of a smile, a raised eyebrow and roll of the eyes caressing her face. We knew that this would be something that we would have to discover for ourselves in our own time.

There were moments that I interpreted as her letting go. She would speak someone's name, then say with a tone of finality and completion as a statement, rather than a question: "Forget it! What's the point?"

I noticed that the names she called were of people with whom she had issues, like my ex-husband. Long, deep sigh. "Aah, forget it! What's the point?"

All those years, as he and I had traversed our marriage, separation and then divorce, she had loved, supported and cared, without a word of condemnation or judgement uttered. Ensconced in my own drama, I did not see that the bond of the womb was not broken. The umbilical pain of her daughter's desperate attempts to hold her life and family together was hers. But there was no point anymore, if ever there was.

One morning, in the pre-dawn darkness, there was a moment of deep connection between us. The previous evening, I had asked:

"Would you like me to make coffee for you, Mummy?" She loved my coffee, looking forward to her first cup before breakfast whenever she visited my home. Surely, I thought, my love-infused brew would give her the caffeine jolt to bring her back to us, to stay with us a little longer, maybe even for next Christmas as Victoria so wanted.

"Yes, that would be nice," she whispered.

The next morning, I lugged my espresso machine and drove the 15 minutes to her townhouse to brew the perfect cup. Cynthia, her favourite nurse, peeled open the front door and unlocked the grille.

"She's still sleeping," she said, voice as quiet as the morning.

I unpacked and set up the machine, measured the Blue Mountain coffee beans into the grinder, buzzing them into a fine grind, tapped the grounds into the cup, poured the water from the Brita pitcher on her kitchen counter and tipped it into the canister of the machine. My ears were on guard for movement on the wooden floor above my head that would indicate that my activity had awakened her. The coffee exploded into the carafe. I reached for her favourite mug, the one with "I ♥ Grandma", and poured the thick love-brew. Then a mug for me, any mug would do, filled to the brim.

It might be a long morning.

I climbed the wooden stairs, the creak of each step sounding like thunder to me, the coffee steaming to warm my face. Her eyes were closed as I entered her room. I sat on the stool beside her bed, my mug in my palms, as if holding my love for her; the mug for her on the bedside table. Mummy lay, awake now, the bed nestling her shrinking body, both of us in silence. An hour vaporised, like the heat of the coffee, cooling, cooling, now cold.

Mummy uttered only: "Daddy."

So much meaning for me in that one word as Mummy and I had endured excruciating experiences with my father when I was running the family business decades earlier. Three and a half years of pain, hurt and sorrow for both of us as her husband, my father, fought us and imperilled the good of the business and our family, for his own reasons that no-one but he could know. All this, long forgiven yet not forgotten, encompassed in that one word "Daddy." The unsaid "Forget it! What's the point?"

Then came the moment when she was sure that it was time. She had been admitted to the University Hospital of the West Indies for a week to stabilise a respiratory complication. On her third morning there, she summoned Carole and me with urgency:

"Well, this is it. Sorry Doug is not here."

"You think we should call him?" I whispered to Carole, wondering how to relay the news to our brother, Doug, of his mother's looming death across five time zones, 8,285 miles from Jamaica to Ghana which he was visiting on business.

"I don't know. What do you think?"

"Well, if it were me, I would want to know. Now!"

We called our brother, the CEO of a major company, the one who made hundreds of decisions every day:

"Should I come home?" His voice begged us to decide for him. Telling him it was his decision to make was futile.

"Yes. Come."

And so, he did, with none of us sure how much longer she would be with us. But she changed her mind about leaving then, and decided to wait for her beloved son, her firstborn. Besides, she had always declared that she wanted to die in her home, not in a hospital. This was not to be "it".

There were moments of impatience, nestled so frail on the edge of her bed, limbs like sticks, the now inevitable sigh shunted from deep within her weakened state, as she made this seemingly ludicrous statement:

"This thing is taking too long. I didn't know it would take so long and be so difficult."

"What thing Mummy?" one of us would ask.

"This transitioning thing. It's taking too long."

And I, or Carole, or Rev. John would chuckle:

"Don't worry. It will soon happen." We laughed, for how crazy it seemed for someone to be wanting this thing, death, that most humans fear.

Then, release, one week before her transition when

A BEAUTIFUL DYING

I was visiting her one Sunday afternoon. I perched beside her on her bed, which she did not leave anymore. Her body was wizened, shrinking, fading away. She spoke the names of the special people to whom we should give her treasures — the tea set for her niece, Maureen, the only one in New York to own her home; a ring for her cousin, Brinnel, who had been a bedrock throughout her life; the china cabinet for Michéle, her beloved daughter-in-law. I grabbed a yellow notepad "Hold on Mummy while I get this down." I scribbled detailed notes as we continued our conversation, like the many times when I had helped her prepare for her overseas travels. She dictated the details of her Service of Thanksgiving:

"I want cheerful colours. I want Pauline to sing. And I want "Love Divine All Loves Excelling" on the program. We used to sing that at morning devotion at Wolmer's you know." Wolmer's was her high school, the cradle of intergenerational memories, the school of my siblings and me as well. It was a joy for me to do this for her, to help her to let go of her personal possessions and to choreograph her final curtain call.

And then on Monday afternoon, the day after

Mother's Day, 44 days after that first glimpse of her dying, Cynthia phoned:

"Come now."

And we knew she was gone, even as we raced to her bedside, hoping to catch her breath, to bid her final farewell. She passed at home in her own bed as she had always wanted. She didn't wait for us. Perhaps it's easier to leave when your loved ones are not around.

A beautiful dying. Watching Mummy taking her time to cross over and discovering it is not something to be feared. Witnessing her process and knowing that death is life and life is death. I recalled her words to me many years before: "You know, Marguerite. Just as how loving arms are here to greet us at birth, surely there must be loving arms to greet us when we die." With that belief, she embraced the process of dying and greeted death when she was ready.

The day after she passed, my siblings and I met with Rev. John to plan her Service of Thanksgiving.

"So, what do we do for the service?" my brother asked.

"It's all here," I replied, handing him the yellow note pad.

We followed her instructions. The church was

a rainbow of family, friends, business associates, people who knew her only as Doug's, Marguerite's or Carole's mother. I wore orange, Carole wore turquoise. Pauline sang. There was even a gaggle of girls in their aquamarine Wolmer's uniforms to pay homage to a loyal "old girl".

"This service felt more like a wedding than a funeral. It was so happy," Jean, a family friend whispered to me as the church emptied.

2

I KEEP LOSING DIAMOND EARRINGS

What a fi yu, cyaan be un fi yu.

I raise my fingers to my left earlobe. My diamond earring. It's not there!

I am on the dance floor at a midsummer dance in Toronto, jigging to the live band when I had felt something fall to my left foot. Still dancing, slower now, I lean over and peer closer to the ground.

"What's wrong?" my friend who had invited me asks.

"I lost my earring."

"What does it look like?"

"It's a diamond solitaire," I respond as I pivot my right ear to show her the bereft other half of the pair.

One by one, other friends on the dance floor lean

I KEEP LOSING DIAMOND EARRINGS

forward and peer to the ground, still dancing. Rose, another friend sidles up to us:

"But wait. Is this some new Jamaican dance?"

"No," I reply, relaying the news of the earring. She joins in the choreography.

A jumble of thoughts goes through my head as I and others search for the earring. I had decided to wear the family heirloom passed from my grandmother to my mother, and now owned jointly by my sister and me. I was tired of seeing them nestled in the maroon velvet jewellery box tucked in my lingerie drawer. What's the sense of having something valuable if you don't enjoy it, I had reasoned. But how do I tell my sister that one of the pair is gone? I resolve that the next day I will give her the remaining earring. It's hers.

I march to the table where I had been sitting and check my place setting, flipping up the blue table cloth and patting the carpeted floor. Nothing there. I return to the dance floor to continue my panicked looking. I tell one of the organisers, hoping that she will ask the band to stop playing right now so that all 500 people on the dance floor can search for the earring. Not a chance.

Throughout, with each breath, I repeat: "Nothing is ever lost." This is what we do in my family whenever we cannot find something. At the least, it calms me. I head back to the table and there is my friend's husband sitting fiddling with his camera. He is a financial guru, one of the people of whom others whisper: "Anything he touches turns to gold." He doesn't like to dance.

"What are you looking for?" he asks.

"I can't find one of my earrings. I think it fell on the dance floor, but I don't see it anywhere."

"You looked under the chairs and table?"

"Yes, I searched everywhere."

He leans over, parts the tablecloth and declares: "See it here!"

And there is the earring, on the floor beside his camera bag.

In my moment of relief, as I tuck the earring into the inner zippered pocket of my evening purse, sealing it with gratitude, this strange thought goes through my mind — how interesting that despite at least seven of us searching for the earring for over an hour, it took a very wealthy man seconds to find it.

I KEEP LOSING DIAMOND EARRINGS

~

One summer Saturday afternoon, two years after that summer ball, I rushed around my home in Toronto. I had invited a friend over for dinner and, as is my wont, had left preparations until the very last minute. In a whirlwind of busyness, I was designing the menu, cleaning the house, shopping for groceries and wine and preparing the meal. With not much time before my guest arrived, I bounded up the stairs to shower and get dressed. As I hauled my sweater over my head, I felt the absence of the diamond earring in my left ear.

My mother, on her deathbed, had handed me her double-diamond ring. It too, along with the diamond solitaire earrings, had been bequeathed to her decades before by Clara, her beloved mother-in-law and my grandmother, in gratitude for her love and caring. This jewel was precious in the invaluable currency of a family history of love. I yearned to wear it more often, but I knew I wouldn't in its current form. I am not a "ring person" so I had not worn it since Mummy's passing, except for a few formal occasions. On one of my trips to Jamaica from my new home in Canada, I had consulted my jeweller who recast it as a pair of earrings, each diamond nestled in a gold crescent, that I now wore all the time.

Shower abandoned, I sank to the floor, squinting for what I hoped would be the glitter of the lost diamond. I retraced each step down the stairs, to the kitchen, laundry, and living room, eyes peeled to no avail. With the arrival of my guest imminent, and I still sweaty and ruffled, I affirmed "Nothing is ever lost. Everything is in its right and perfect place," as my mother, Daisy, used to say. It had worked with the diamond earring at the dance. Would it work its magic again? I e-mailed my sister, Rev. John and Carol, the jeweller, asking them to pray for the reappearance of the earring. They joined me in the affirmation. Carol even added a tad of humour: "Daisy must have borrowed it for some hot date up in heaven. She'll soon return it." I managed a smile through my clenched teeth.

Over the next few days, I traversed my home head down, eyes scanning every corner and crease in the floor. I asked my three doggies if they had seen the earring: "No. But don't worry," their wagging tails seemed to say. I let go of the searching and

I KEEP LOSING DIAMOND EARRINGS

the worrying. I kept affirming "Nothing is ever lost."

But I had a problem — what would my "go to" daily wear earrings now be? I felt lost without them. I was even about to buy a new pair when I was at the airport in Antigua a few weeks later returning from a client assignment. For some reason, I didn't. Five weeks after losing the earring, I was at the checkout at Loblaw's supermarket. I opened my reusable bag to pack the groceries, and there was the earring.

It was my niece's wedding day. As I dressed for the occasion that May afternoon in Jamaica, I removed my "go to" diamond earrings, one of which I had lost and found years before in Loblaw's. I lifted the diamond solitaire heirlooms from their maroon velvet box, one of which I had lost and found at the summer ball and inserted them into my earlobes. I hesitated, as I wondered if I might lose one again, remembering the superstition that bad things always happen in threes. Then I let the thought go, knowing that nothing is ever lost. But just in case, as I headed out the front door, I said to my sister:

"Carole. Please check the backs of the earrings."

And later, as we danced at the reception, she sidled up to me:

"Just checking that the earrings are still on."

They were.

Letting go does not mean giving up. I had let go of my attachment to the earrings because, whilst they are of sentimental value, they are things. The real value is in the memories of my relationship with my mummy and my grandma which were in no way diminished by the loss of the earrings. Yet, I never gave up that they would reappear. Sometimes magic happens and the thing that I thought was lost, returns. Or maybe it is never found, at least not by me. It is just in its right and perfect place.

3

THE MAIDEN AUNT

What goat do, kid follow.

"Every family needs a maiden aunt," my mother often declared, as she spoke of Winnie, her eldest sister.

The black rotary phone tucked in the corner of the passage at Littledene, the name of my childhood home on Braemar Avenue in Kingston Jamaica, would ring every morning. Unless Daddy had once again upset a client, it would herald Auntie Winnie's voice like the riff of a piano interlude: "How is the morrrnning", stretching "morning" into four syllables, three notes. She always said that, no matter who answered, like a bird welcoming the day with its song. "Gigi," my brother, Douglas, called her, from a little ditty he had made up as a five-year old, when he spent afternoons with her and our grandparents whilst Mummy and Daddy were at work.

One morning, when Winnie was three years old, she had awakened and cried out "Mama! I can't move!" Polio left her with one leg shorter, half as thick and the foot two sizes smaller than the other. Those were the days when people with disabilities were called "cripples", told they couldn't do this, or that and were made to stay home, out of sight. But not little Winnie. She went to school, earned her accounting qualifications, became a teacher, excelled at music. There was even talk of the young Winnie having had a romance with a minister who wanted to marry her. But her parents said no. So, our maiden aunt she became.

The toot-toot of the horn in our driveway at 7.15 a.m. every school morning signalled to my sister, Carole, and me and our cousins, Terri and Andi, to move out the door like sprinters shooting from the starting blocks. Because Auntie Winnie would not tarry, lest we make her late for her students at the Kingston Technical High School. And at any rate, we certainly didn't want to miss seeing the cute guy on the corner whom we passed every day waiting for his bus as her Hillman Minx crawled down Lady Musgrave Road. A teacher all her life, she managed to not only survive but thrive on her pittance of a salary. Auntie Winnie learned that by folding a large swath of African print, stitching the sides and cutting a circle in the middle she could create cool, elegant dresses. Her "1-2-3-4" recipe for pound cake and Easter buns made with beer instead of yeast were delights to us, gifts made with love at very little cost. She paid for Carole and me to accompany Mummy and Daddy to Scotland for our brother's graduation from university. Many a fortnight she was the saviour in covering the payroll at my parents' business. She travelled each summer on her own to visit her sister, Perle, in Alaska; her brother, Roy, and his wife, Irene, in Saskatoon, her dear friends, Fran and Lee, in Buffalo and Sally in Florida.

Each weekday morning at 10.00 a.m. the hymn, "Jesu, Joy of Man's Desiring", would waft from the radio. The announcer would introduce the program, adding, "produced and hosted by Lloyd Hall with Miss Winnifred Ebanks on piano". We attended Easter and Christmas concerts at the St. Andrew Scots Kirk Presbyterian Church on Duke Street in downtown Kingston with the St. Andrew Singers, voices raised to the heavenly heights of the cavernous ceiling of the church, framed by the organ with pipes like fingers reaching to God, the back of Mr. Hall's balding head at the organ or conducting, all accompanied by the sure and steady comfort of "Miss Winnifred Ebanks, Pianoforte".

Most of all, Winnie was a rock for Daisy, my mother — a shoulder to cry on, an ear to listen, a refuge from the tumult of her marriage, a sister-mother for her children. "Our family's maiden aunt", Mummy would say. In the latter years of their retirement, she and Mummy gathered each afternoon at the antique dining table at Winnie's town home in Devon Square, sipping tea from her best English Bone China. Daisy would lean back, one arm draped over the back of the chair, the other on the table, open to whatever wisdom her big sister was about to emit. Winnie, twirling her thumbs would say: "Then Daisy . . .", and off she would go with sage words, an insightful question or a naughty joke, like blessings flowing from a mountain spring.

THE MAIDEN AUNT

Dear Auntie Winnie, Gigi — such a beautiful soul. Is there anyone who did not love her? Perhaps the boyfriends of her students, for whom she only wanted the best. Threats to "lef mi woman alone" hastened her exit from the classroom. No-nonsense Auntie Winnie, who would never be late for school, would not allow some "ghetto youth" to dictate her life.

She was a woman of great faith in the Divine, stalwart of the United Church, an elder and practitioner of Christ-principles. I could never understand how church people could quarrel so as I eavesdropped on conversations between her and my father, discussing what went on in the church. I remember her once reporting that she had just listened to the discussions at the church synod and then interjected in the pause: "Now gentlemen, what would Jesus do?" She was the only woman in the group, laying the foundation of strength and independence for the girls in our family, before the women's movement, before feminism became a thing.

4

NO-ONE EVER WANTS THE BOTTOM BUNK

Family stick wi bend but it won' bruk.

In days to come, the bunk bed would be a castle, a cave, an igloo. Today, it stands in the middle of our bedroom as a monument to Aunt Dottie's deathbed appeal to my father: "Take care of the children for me."

My sister, Carole, and I have played hide and seek, tag-you're-it, Simon Says in our room. Cotton sheets, faded with time, and weekly laundering cover the two beds that have seen trampoline competitions and pillow fights and have been our refuge, the musty space beneath providing haven from sibling teasing or parental punishment. Now they are stacked like Lego blocks to create space. We share an old, some say antique, but it's just old, dresser with four drawers, two for each of us. Today there's a second dresser, scrambled from Auntie Winnie's garage, that Mr. Russell, the painter, had slathered in buttercup yellow earlier that week. It's jammed beneath the wooden sash window through which orange and grapefruit trees peer, enveloping us with the scent of bee-covered buds. It will be a good harvest this year. The wooden floorboards ache with the weight of additional furniture, limiting the space for our board games and Barbies. Your cousins will share your room, my sister and I have been told.

We awaken before dawn, willing their arrival as we have done when our dog, Sheba, looked ready to birth her puppies. We race to the front door at the intermittent grind of cars forging down Braemar Avenue, same as we did with each of Sheba's contractions. No puppies yet. No car. We slump with disappointment as the cars accelerate past our gate fading away to the Soares at #5, the Cumpers at #3, the horse pasture at the end of the road. Maybe if we wait in the tree house they will come quicker, we reason. Like the little lizards that populate our garden, we scuttle up the trunk of the mango tree at the rear of the driveway. My sister wonders what the cousins will be like. "Probably weird", I blurt. Between the leaves and the young fruit, we catch sight of darkening clouds rising from behind Jack's Hill. Bertha, the cook, summons us inside, lest rain falls. But it doesn't, and we crave doing something, anything, to make the time of their arrival come sooner.

Daddy's white 1960 Chevrolet finally curves into the driveway, halting at the front landing sentinelled by cactus plants and a concrete bench. Mummy opens the rear right door, lunging her arms to coax little Andrea from the car. She's only eighteen months old. Theresa, all of six years, has already slithered out the other side. It's been an interminable flight from New York, still embraced in winter, to this land where summer never ends. Their eyes bulge at the sight of this new place, and of strange adults with pitying eyes and patting hands. Poor things. They have lost their mother. Welcome to Jamaica and your new home.

We dine together that evening at the large

mahogany table, used only for special occasions. Daddy asks me to say the grace.

"Thank you God for food to eat amen."

"No. Say it again", Daddy instructs.

I do. He insists that I repeat it, and I can't figure out why. Then he takes over and adds: "And thank you for bringing Theresa and Andrea safely to our home." Sure wish he had explained that he wanted this little extra thanksgiving, I think, as my body slouches with embarrassment.

By bedtime, a little later than usual with the flurry, the novelty of this day, Theresa and Andrea are Terri and Andi. Their clothes, emitting the stale smell of the city as they were released from stuffed suitcases, have been squirreled away in the buttercup yellow dresser. Two pairs of sisters giggle as we snuggle into each other on the top bunk, the bottom bed empty. No one ever wants the bottom bunk. Too young to understand all that has taken place in the last two months, and all that yet will, like toy soldiers we cascade into sleep. As I drift away, Terri's silky ponytail draped over my arm, I wonder: would having to share my bedroom also mean that I have to share my parents?

5

MY FATHER'S BOSS

Every long lane 'ave a turnin'.

"Oh God Oh God Oh God!" wailed my father, pacing in and out of my office like a lost dog, breath tight in his throat, his palms cupping his temple.

"I didn't know, Daddy. I didn't know," I whispered through the confusion and fear of an animal cornered. I had just agreed to pay our workers for the time they were on strike.

"You never do that," Daddy moaned. How was I to know?

The strike was over. Mr Williams, the rotund union representative had led his delegates in a victory parade out of my office, down the stairs to the factory floor. With them went the scent of cedar dust nestled like snow on the boots of the workers' delegates, Fennell and Morgan. With them went any illusion that this would be a happy experience.

The week before, my brother had departed Jamaica for Boston to pursue his MBA at Harvard Business School. After eight years successfully managing our family's business, he handed the baton to me. "I think you are the best person to run the business," he had said six months before when he received his acceptance from Harvard. Who says no to their big brother? I was twenty-three years old (but my round face said sixteen) five feet tall, less than a year out of university. And I was now the boss of seventy of the most hardened, barely literate, but highly skilled woodworkers who created doors in the factory owned by my family. I was also my father's boss.

Five years prior to my birth, my father had been fired from his job as a supervisor at Abraham Henriques and Joy, a leading building construction firm in Jamaica. He cocooned himself at home for three weeks and then emerged to start his own construction business, reminding my mother of her marriage vows "for richer, for poorer, for better, for worse". I don't think she ever forgave him for having to abandon her career in insurance. The woman who replaced her rose to the pinnacle of the industry in Jamaica. My mother always wondered – "Could that have been me"?

They started operations in a converted residence on Gold Street in downtown Kingston. The aged wooden dwelling house became the administrative office; corrugated zinc sheets covered the paved backyard to shelter the hodgepodge of lumber, plywood, machinery and equipment. At some point, they exited building construction to specialise in the manufacture of wooden doors and the installation of sliding doors. My sister and I worked there in summer holidays and after school, counting money, collating the payroll, filing, typing. The sharp, sweet aroma of cedar and the incessant whirring of band saws, jointers and lathes are etched in the backdrop of my childhood. Until my brother took over after his return from university, the business was at best marginal and at worst teetering on the edge, kept alive by my father's unwavering commitment to quality and service and my mother's astute money juggling. Yet, it provided a comfortable, carefree childhood for my older brother, younger sister and me, including the very best education and even a few summer vacations abroad.

I graduated from the University of the West Indies with an honours degree in Management, my experience in the family business positioning me ahead of my classmates. I worked for six months in an entry level position at a prominent firm in Jamaica, until I got that call from my brother. I thought I knew so much from university: marketing, accounting, finance, operations, business law, organisational behaviour. But books, projects and classes, lecturers with doctorates and little practical experience provided only a scrap of what I would now need. The wellbeing of my entire family was at stake, as our family home was mortgaged to the hilt and my parents' personal assets pledged fully to the bank. The livelihood of seventy employees, their children and spouses, depended on my every decision. Mr Stephenson, a staple in my life who had picked me up from school every day of my childhood in a battered pickup, now looked to me for his weekly salary. Miss Sybil, the cleaner, with whose children I had played, trusted me that her children would not go hungry.

FORGET IT! WHAT'S THE POINT?

There were Fridays when the payroll couldn't be met, where within thirty minutes of signing the pay cheques with a pen of hope, I would drive to the bank. Seated in the manager's office, I lay a sheet of paper before him:

"Here are our Accounts Receivables. We should collect these in the next week," pointing to the names of three or four customers. "We need a temporary line of credit to tide us over."

"Sure. No problem," Mr Sharpe, the bank manager would say. I could now enjoy the weekend. I learned that it is best to be open and honest with your creditors, and to share bad news early. I learned to ask, even when afraid of what the answer might be.

Three and a half years of darkness roiled. Another strike, threats of strikes; a stagnating economy; social decay. There was a larger global context: Jamaica, ninety miles south of Cuba, was important then to the USA during the 1970s, when the Cold War between that country and the Soviet Union was raging. We were collateral damage, a staging ground for the East vs. West conflict. And our local political parties mirrored this by taking sides, which played out in violence and mayhem in our daily lives. By then, we had relocated the factory to Nanse Pen, an industrial estate to the west of Kingston. I remember one afternoon driving back to the factory from a meeting, my passage thwarted by a large crowd gathered in the neighbouring open lot. The police had shot and killed two men, whose bodies were now splayed in the bushes, gawked at by children too young for school, unemployed youths and young women ripe with babies. At the height of the unrest, or what we called "the war", our employees would come to work exhausted from nights when the roar of gunfire had outmanoeuvred sleep. Up all night keeping watch, their bodies would often succumb to slumber on benches, in secluded corners beneath piles of lumber or even at their machines.

One of our employees, Mr Scott, occupied the Gold Street premises and he would rent out the shed for dances. One Friday night, men armed with machine guns raided one of his dances. Four people were murdered in what is infamous as the Gold Street Massacre. Trying to gain entry, the gunmen pushed the doors to the house where Mr Scott and his family cowered beneath their beds. The only thing that saved them was my father's obsession with sliding doors: all the doors in the house slid sideways on tracks rather than opening inward on hinges.

But the worst experience in this very trying period, was the betrayal by my father. Arguments, his constant questioning, second-guessing and undermining of my decisions resulted in employees taking sides, pitting us against each other like children in their parents' divorce. My mother became the referee of mammoth fights between her obstinate husband and equally resolute daughter. He was always right, and so was I. The stress aged her, sickened her, driving her to Dr Mendes, our family doctor and friend, on more than one occasion. On my brother's recommendation, I had moved out of my parents' home into my own townhouse. It became my refuge for sanity and recovery from the torment of the business and my father. My cat Chaillot hugged my sorrows and tears the way cats do, curled tight, unperturbed by the foibles of the human world. The darkness threatened to shatter our family, our wealth and our future beyond repair.

In 1983, the perfect storm: the business was doing well, my parents were at retirement age and I wanted to further my education. The interest of

MY FATHER'S BOSS

a large customer in vertical integration presented an opportunity to sell the business. We took it. My parents were free to retire, and I to pursue my MBA. More importantly, we were able to begin the healing of our family. But the darkness remained in my heart for a long time: anger at my father, unforgiveness of the employees who had made those years difficult, even guilt at abandoning those who had been loyal. Yet deep within, I would remember the story my mother often told that shortly after my birth, at the lowest moment in the business when bankruptcy loomed, I was her joy. She would nurture, feed, care for and play with me, all the while saying: "You are my little sunshine. They can take away everything from me. But they can't take you away." And I would gurgle and coo, as babies do so perfectly, with not a care in the world. And I recalled numerous school prizegiving ceremonies, sports days, ballet concerts, music recitals, every one of which Daddy viewed through the lens of his Alpa camera. I knew that I was loved by my mother and my father.

Within a few years, the new owners ran the business into the ground. The building through which my father lived the architect dream of his youth fell to ruins, overgrown with bushes, now trees. Every now and then, travelling around Kingston, I would hear someone call "Miss Orane. You remember me?" And I would smile and hug my former employee.

"Why did you sell your family's business?" people still ask, decades later. I never answer.

6

A CHANCE ENCOUNTER WITH A PIPE

Di deeper yuh dig, di richer di soil.

"May we sit here?" I asked the grey-bearded gentleman perched on a ledge between two shipping containers that housed the Visa office and the McDonald's restaurant at the Barra Olympic Park in Rio de Janeiro. My brother, Douglas, sister-in-law, Michéle, and I needed a break from the scorching Brazilian sun.

"I hope you don't mind the pipe," he responded, easing it from between his teeth, his face open and smiling just in case we really did not mind the pipe.

There are few things to which I apply the word

"hate". Smoking is one of them. I cross the street to avoid a cigarette smoker, making sure not to hide my chiding eyes and rebuking lips. I don't own an ashtray. I grapple with compassion for people made sick by smoking. "Actually, I love it. It reminds me of my grandfather," I exhaled as I succumbed to memories of my childhood. Doug, Michéle and I sank to the ledge, grateful for any seat in the park teeming with the world at the Rio 2016 Olympic Games.

Grandpa died when I was seven years old. Perhaps because I have so few memories, the scent of pipe tobacco wafts powerfully in my heart. Grandpa sitting in his wheelchair on the fern-fringed verandah of the family home, his pipe lodged between his lips, me playing on the floor in the space left vacant by the amputation of one diabetic leg. He would extend his bamboo cane, hooking it around my neck to pull me to his lap. His chuckle bypassed the pipe at the corner of his mouth to meet my mirth as I drew towards him. He is the only grandparent I remember. Gray hair, wrinkled skin, the amputated leg, his joy in his little granddaughter. And the pipe.

"Where are you from?" the gentleman asked, in tentative English.

A CHANCE ENCOUNTER WITH A PIPE

"Jamaica," we responded together.

His body straightened, his eyes sparkled: "I love Jamaica. I remember seeing that movie about the Jamaican bobsled team."

"Yes. *Cool Runnings*."

"Right. And I said I had to go there. So, I went for four days and stayed for three weeks." He laughed, a joyful clap, secret memories sparking his eyelids.

Doug, Michéle and I smiled. It's a common story you hear, when you are Jamaican.

"I went all over the island. And I visited a few more times with my wife and children. I told them they had to see this place. I want my grandchildren to go there one day too." He had even visited the synagogue in Jamaica. "I found the Jews there very stuck-up." We chuckled, tempted to ask who he had met, sure that we know them. "But I loved the ordinary Jamaican people." We know lots of those too.

"Where are you from?" my turn to ask, not able to place his accent.

"Israel."

"Israel! I have been trying to convince my wife to visit, but she won't go. Can you please tell her that it's safe?" pleaded my brother.

– 39 –

FORGET IT! WHAT'S THE POINT?

The pipe smoker launched into his family's history in Israel from 1510, the dispersion of the Jews throughout the centuries, his travels to other places in the world, and what it's really like living there, despite the existence of Palestine, his tone suggesting that he disputed their right to exist. I was tempted to point out that the Bible speaks of the state of Palestine, but had no desire to get involved in that conflict. It was too sunny a day. He also loved the ordinary Iranian, Jordanian and Syrian, and assured us that we would love the ordinary Israeli too. I wondered if he was a Mossad spy, the places he had visited, the wry smile on his face betraying intimate knowledge of places normally hidden from his people.

"I'm reading a book about Israel," my sister-in-law interjected.

"Oh? What book?"

"Can't quite remember the author." She shuffled around in her bag and minutes later proffered her phone with the googled information: "To the End of the Land."

"Oh, that's by David Grossman. He's a personal friend of mine."

A CHANCE ENCOUNTER WITH A PIPE

We all marvelled at the smallness of the world.

He and my brother competed for bragging rights as they listed previous Olympics they had attended. They had both been to Atlanta and Sydney. He was at Rio to see Usain Bolt, our star Jamaican athlete. Who wasn't at the Rio Olympics to see Bolt, we wondered, judging from the celebrity status we enjoyed just by being Jamaican? He wanted to know more about Bolt, why Jamaicans run so fast, how long we would be in Rio and what events we planned to see. We filled him in on Bolt's upbringing, how humble his parents are, and what a lovely young man he is. We shared a brief history of athletics in Jamaica, and what we think makes Jamaicans run so fast. We told him we would see all of Bolt's races as well as swimming, diving, volleyball, gymnastics, equestrian, Taekwondo. He lamented that he was only able to get tickets for the 200-metre sprint final, but that would be enough. He just wanted to see Bolt, the "The Big Man," run.

"You must all come to Israel," he instructed. "It's perfectly safe. Don't listen to the media. E-mail me and you can come visit. My wife and I, our children are grown and have left home, so we have the whole upper floor. You can stay with us and I will show you around. It's always best when you know someone who lives there." He scratched his email address on my McDonald's receipt.

How different this experience might have been had the pipe bothered me. I made a friend, I learned things I did not know, both historical and current. I thought about the strangeness of life — of all the places we could have sat in that expansive Olympic Park, we chose the one next to a pipe-smoking Israeli grandpa, who reminded us of our grandpa, who loves Jamaica and is a personal friend of an author of a book one of us is currently reading.

I emailed him that evening, already planning the itinerary for my trip to Israel. I have yet to receive a reply.

7

CROWNING GLORY

Who di cap fit, let dem wear it.

"Marguerite!" my mother bellowed from her bedroom. "Please come here now."

"What is it Mummy?" annoyed that she was interrupting whatever I was doing, yet hearing desperation in her voice. I entered the bedroom and stopped a few steps in. Carole, my eleven-year-old sister was in a knot on my parents' bed, her face wet with tears, each sob emitting a fresh flow. Daddy was standing like the concrete post at our gate, his back to her. Mummy, like the concrete post on the other side, stood before him. Neither moved. There was a war going on.

"Please speak to your father."

Oh dear, I thought to myself. This is bad when I am to speak to "your father" and not Daddy.

"Carole wants to cut her hair and he refuses to let her." She continued.

"Hair is a woman's crowning glory!" my father declared, each syllable louder and higher, so that "glory" ended like the screech of one of the parakeets that visited the fruit trees in our backyard.

Funny, I thought, you had no problem with me cutting my hair four years ago.

"Well, it's her hair," I declared with the fullness of my fourteen-year-old feminist fury. "She can do whatever she wants with it."

He stalked out of the room, repeating his crowning glory mantra, realising that he had lost this battle. Later that afternoon, Carole cut her hair to reveal a curly pixie cut. She bounded in the house, light and happy.

Growing up in Jamaica, it was a rite of passage somewhere around puberty, for black girls to cut their "doo-doo plaits". This was not just a hairstyle change, it was liberation from weekly washing and combing. Each Saturday, I would sit on the floor,

Mummy seated on the edge of the bed, her knees like clamps around my body, so I could not move as she tore the comb through the knots and kinks of my voluminous hair, sopping wet, because that much hair takes a long time to dry. Tears were common, screams even, as I pressed my palms against my scalp, to anaesthetise the pain. Getting rid of the braids meant we would be free from scraping our hair into buns for ballet class, brushing like ironing to get the kinks to lay flat. Not to mention trying to fit all that hair into a swim cap for swimming class! And we just ached to stop looking like children, as our little bodies started to spurt the signs of womanhood.

Carole and I had different hair experiences. Since Christopher Columbus had landed in Jamaica in 1492, people from all corners of the world – England, Europe, China, India, the Middle East came to seek their fortune there, lured by the promise of wealth based on the "free" labour of Africans hauled across the Atlantic to be enslaved. The result is a mixed population where our ancestry is telegraphed by the colour of our skin and the texture of our hair. When you are mixed, and your babies are born, you never know what the melting pot will serve. Carole, with her silky black hair in light curls, was often asked if she was from India. There was no mistaking what my ancestry was — my kinky hair confirmed that our ancestors had indeed crossed the Middle Passage from West Africa to Jamaica. Daddy's crowning glory declaration applied to Carole, but not to me, reflecting the view that African hair is bad, and straight hair is good. I picture the European slave traders gazing in wonder at my ancestors whom they had captured and dragged to the West African coast, semi-naked, dirty, hungry but with hair like crowns. "Oh no," I imagine them saying, "This looks too much like royalty. That crown must go." And so, my ancestors' hair was shorn. But hair grows back, so the hair had to be made to be despised, lest they really did remember their regal roots.

My African hair journey took me from "doo-doo plaits" to relaxing, the most oxymoronic term ever, since there was nothing relaxing about the experience. Every two months, I spent three to four hours at Mummy's hairdresser on Half Way Tree Road. I wanted so much to look like the ladies as they left the salon, with their black, silky, lightly curled hair, sculpted to perfection with hair spray but with not a kink in sight. Mrs Morales, the hairdresser, would smear Vaseline on the skin around my hairline to avoid chemical burns. Then she would comb an entire jar of Jaffrey's Hair Straightener through my kinks, each scratch of the comb digging the chemical into my scalp. Because bad hair is stubborn, I then had to sit for twenty minutes with my scalp on chemical fire, the hairdresser checking my skin every few minutes to smear more Vaseline on my burning flesh. The relief of the shampoo and rinse was superseded only by joy at witnessing my hair hanging down my back straight as a light pole. That wasn't the end though as the hair had to be curled on metal rollers and set under the hood dryer for two hours. It took that long to dry, because my hair was straight, but still very, very thick.

Black power and Angela Davis brought me true hair liberation in 1972. I was sixteen. I cut the straightness off, and my hair bounced into a natural, kinky halo — an Afro! Well-meaning aunts and teachers asked me why I was spoiling my "good-good hair." And I almost made the news, when my high school principal, Miss Pinto, a draconian spinster with short, straight hair, whose ancestors were reputed to have been Portuguese Jews who had fled the Inquisition, threatened to ban all Afro-wearing girls from the annual prize giving. The press gathered at the National Arena where the function was being held, but there was no news, as Miss Pinto had backtracked. I waltzed into the function to accept my prize, proud of my Afro crown.

But hair grows. And so, there's always this question of "What do I do with my hair?" If I wanted it long and natural, it would be back to the torturous comb-through. I could relax again, but going through that agony was unthinkable. Plus, becoming more health conscious, I wondered how healthy it could be to subject one's scalp, the casing for the brain, to such chemical terror. But more liberation came with the elevation of cane rows, the intricate braiding patterns that my ancestors brought with them from Africa, that had been signs of shame, but were now once again recognised as signs of beauty. I loved cane rows and was blessed that my friend, Elsa, was a master at it. Every two weeks, I would sit at her feet, her nimble fingers parting, braiding and sculpting my hair into works of art as we chatted and laughed.

I tried other people's hair — braid extensions and

even a weave. The hair felt heavy and jerked my neck back when I ran or danced. I read about the billion-dollar hair industry, fuelled by the desperation of women in India and China who grew and then sold their locks to feed their families. I wanted no such karma on my head.

Along the way, I met Carolyn, a Vidal-Sassoon trained, white Jamaican whose philosophy was simple: "Your hair is to serve you, not the other way around." Her only tool was a pair of scissors. No hair dryer, chemicals, curling iron or blow-dryer. She shampooed my hair, I sat in her chair, she cut, fluffed with her fingers and off I went, knowing that her mastery ensured hassle-free natural hair until the next appointment.

My quest to have a crowning glory brought me to locks. For the last seventeen years, I have had hundreds of rope-like threads cascading down my back that always looks spectacular.

"Are those braids?" I am asked.

"No. Think of Bob Marley's dreadlocks, but not as thick."

"How long does it take to do your hair?" a sixty-something coiffured blond asked me one Saturday in the checkout line at Shopper's Drugmart in Toronto.

"Less time than it takes to do yours."

"I don't believe you," she flung to my departing back, as I floated out of the store on the glory of my hair, wondering if she really thought that I cared whether she believed me or not.

And yes, my hair is all mine, every glorious, kinky, textured strand, resplendent in three dimensions, up, down and sideways, twisted, curled, sculpted to magnificence. Thanks Daddy, for this idea that my hair is my crowning glory.

8

THE ARTIST

Di more yuh chop breadfruit root, di more it spring.

Twenty women and one man filed through the garden at the yoga studio for the painting workshop. Like me, all had done art at school. Snippets of not being considered good at art or being creative darted amongst us as we settled into the open studio embraced by lush tropical foliage, and into our yearning to express ourselves.

We began the class with meditation. A mango tumbled from the tree onto the roof, and then to the ground, a cymbal in the gentle chorus of wind chimes and leaves. We continued to sit in stillness as Denise, our facilitator, shared her journey as an artist. And some of us shared ours. I offered that I had not picked up a brush or paint since leaving school. Many heads nodded in agreement. A few, the more accomplished artists I later learned, lowered their eyes, the corners of their lips seeming to say: "You poor thing."

I recalled a conversation with my thirteen-year-old son the previous week.

"Mummy, how can you be wrong in art?" Shane asked, leaning forward from the rear seat of the car. I had picked him up from school, as I had done for over ten years. I drove down the driveway and through the school gate, the foothills of the Blue Mountains on my left, the city of Kingston to my right, stretching to the harbour and the Caribbean Sea.

"Why do you ask Shane? And please buckle your seatbelt."

"My teacher keeps telling me I am doing it wrong."

"I really don't know Shane. I have always told you that there are no wrong answers, but there are ways to do things better or differently. Maybe that's what your teacher is trying to tell you."

Shane, head still close to mine, nodded.

THE ARTIST

"You know," I continued "in the classes I teach at the university, some of my students have a hard time coming up with ideas for new businesses. They tell me they feel this way because of their experience with art. I tell them that every one of us is creative. I believe that art is a creative expression of our inner being. There can be no right or wrong in art. It is personal."

"Right! I think what I am doing is good. I like it. And my friends think it's good too. But my teacher says I am wrong."

"I know what you mean. I went through this myself when I was at high school."

Shane lurched forward, face almost touching mine eager to hear yet another tale that proved that his mother had once been young. I slowed to the stop sign on Shortwood Road.

"Your seatbelt, Shane. If you don't buckle it now, I will have to stop the car." I heard the seatbelt buckle snap.

"I remember my art teacher, Miss Coke, and how she plucked the paint brush from my hand and completed my final exam piece for me as time was running out."

"You had to take an art exam?"

"Yes, and even with Miss Coke's help, I barely passed. But I loved the classes, because Eliz, my best friend, was in the class and she was really good. That girl could draw! We had fun with the other girls, chatting and laughing. And the art room was right next to the Chemistry lab at the Boys' School, so we got to check out the cute guys."

Shane laughed at the idea of his mother as a giddy sixteen-year-old, ogling boys. I thought of the boys I had eyed and wondered what had happened to them and whether they had aged well.

"Once I left high school, that was it for me and art, and many other things that I had been told I wasn't good at, like Physics, Chemistry and Math."

"I am not good at science or Math too. I don't like them," Shane reminded me, at which point I thought to end the conversation, lest we get into a discussion about there being no right or wrong answers in Math.

"Shane, you just continue to draw, paint and enjoy your art regardless of what your teacher says." As I drove through the Benson Avenue gully, dry at this time of the year, I heard his breathing go quiet, the excitement of his school day, the purr of the car, lulling him to sleep. He jerked awake when we turned into our driveway.

"You know Shane, I am going to do some art classes myself next weekend."

"You are?"

"Yes. There's a workshop at my yoga studio that I signed up for," I said, realising I was speaking to myself as Shane had unbuckled his seatbelt, thrown open the door and jumped out the moment I had stopped the car. I lingered a moment behind the steering wheel, remembering the poster at my yoga studio which read: "Learn how to paint from the heart evoking the beauty hidden within us. Join us as we celebrate the Goddesses within and around us." I had registered, drawn by an urging that whispered:

"Yes Marguerite, time to unleash your inner artist. Time to enjoy art."

Denise set us our first assignment. I stared at the blank canvas perched on the easel, the paint palette and brushes, waiting for me to bring them together.

Others around me began, forms, colours, patterns emerging. My canvas remained blank. My gaze out into the garden rested on the fallen mango, hues of red, orange with a hint of green, nestled in a pot of ferns. My inner artist stirred, like my mouth watering for that mango. I reached for a brush, dipped the point into the orange paint and poised it on the canvas. And like mangoes ripening and tumbling in ever more profusion, my creativity burst from me to land as art. Wending among us, curving between raindrops of words that could hurt and shut us down or uplift and inspire, pointing out what we could have done differently, Denise validated our efforts as coming from our individual hearts, and therefore of value and worth to the world. Smiles, laughter, joy prevailed in abundance as the goddesses created, and the sole gentleman joined in and celebrated.

Soon, too soon, the workshop came to an end. Denise called us to order:

"Let's create a gallery. I have masking tape so you can tape your work on the walls and easels. Then we will all walk around and look at each other's work. Remember to do so with love. Every one of you here is an artist."

THE ARTIST

I appreciated each person's creations, even as I loved my own, recalling Shane's words: "I think what I am doing is good. I like it."

We danced out of the studio, each of us cradling two or three pieces ready for framing. I arrayed my masterpieces on the back seat of the car. Starting the engine, I wound the windows shut and turned the air conditioner to high. I grasped the steering wheel and laughed the car down the driveway exclaiming: "I am an artist!"

I thought of other things I am that others never thought I would be:

"I am an athlete." Whoever thought that Marguerite, who always came last at every sport's day at school, would win an age-group trophy in a road race, as well as medals for finishing marathons?

"I am an author." Whoever thought that Marguerite, who lost the battle with her Management Communications lecturer at business school, and failed the course, would publish a book that people would buy, read and actually like?

"It does not matter what other people think," I declared to myself. "I know I am an artist as gifted as Picasso, Michaelangelo and all the other famous artists throughout history. Whatever the Universe provided them, it provided me. Does it matter to me if anyone agrees? Absolutely not! For I know who I am. I am an artist. Regardless of what anyone has ever told me or tells me now."

I looked forward to showing off my masterpieces to my children, the ultimate truthsayers. As I bubbled closer to home, past the turnoff to their school, I remembered their excitement as little children trundling over each other into the car, vying to be the first to show me their creation. "Mummy! Look what I did in art today. You like it?" jostling with each other to get their masterpieces before my eyes, the fact that I was driving not fazing them in the least. I felt a tinge of trepidation as I stepped out of the car on my arrival home, but this was outweighed by my pride and enthusiasm. I bounded through the front door, bursting to display the works to them.

"Look what I did in art today."

Silence. Victoria, Shane and their friend Daniel continued to stare at the video game screen. I stood, broad smile, arms spread wide, my artwork clothes-pinned in the fingers of each hand, waiting for their approval, but knowing that if I didn't get it, it didn't matter. Their heads swivelled.

"I want one framed for my room!" Victoria declared.

"You did that? It's good!" Shane added.

And Daniel opined "Wow auntie! That is wicked!"

Trust children. I am an artist, giggled every one of the over thirty-seven trillion cells that, according to scientists, make up my body.

9

BUTTERFLY WINGS

Time longer dan rope.

"Victoria. Why do you keep playing with Grandma's arms like that?" I asked my then six-year-old daughter. She and my mother were seated in the antique rocking chair in my living room, Victoria in her lap, legs like a smile caressing her grandma's tummy, thumb of her right hand in her mouth and her left fingers flicking the under flesh of her grandma's left arm. Their heads leaned like two halves of a heart. The rocking chair creaked like a metronome. They were silent. Victoria raised her head and pulled her thumb from her mouth:

BUTTERFLY WINGS

"Is soft," returning her thumb to its place of comfort, the rocking of the chair uninterrupted. Mummy smiled as their heads became one heart again.

That under flesh of a woman's arms is the bane of the fifty-something year old woman. We call them butterfly wings, trying to make light of how our bodies are changing, watching in dismay as they get larger and flappier. Victoria would try to play with my arms, but I hated it. And she didn't like it either. It felt different to grandma's, who was then in her late seventies, and had soft, flapping butterfly wings.

The human body is perfect. Every part, every cell of this intricate temple that encases us on our entire sojourn on planet earth, has its own function and purpose. As a child, my body skipped, ran, jumped, rode bicycles, donkeys and horses, danced, swam, climbed trees, kicked puddles in the rain. It learned ballet, that peculiar art form that isolates and brings attention to each body part and which has been the foundation of all physical activity throughout my life. In high school, my body played hockey, tennis, danced to drums, competed in swim meets, performed dances for tourists, curled in boys' laps. It became something admired by men (and a few women), flesh firm, perky and promising fertility. In later years, my body learned karate, ran marathons, did yoga and Tai Chi, and danced, always dancing. It rocked all night at reggae festivals, and wined and chipped at Carnival in Trinidad. It kept moving.

It carried babies. To have another life within you, and to feel it growing and developing, to see how my own body facilitated this process during and after pregnancy, took my body awareness to another level, starting with the first three months when the life within is a secret, except for the glow of joy and enlarging breasts (at last, I would think). The little bun became a large protrusion cradling the life within. And that life, that body, would swim, twirl, kick, lay still. It would respond to what I ate, what it heard, how I moved. That other body, my child, was the master and dictated when it would enter the world. And when it was time, the order and precision of the birthing process ushered the new life out of my body and into its own earthly experience. My body followed its lead.

My body was now a dairy. It produced milk on

demand. As a student of business, someone who had managed manufacturing plants, I was fascinated by the synchronicity of demand and supply. The baby cried, and I produced the milk. And I produced as long as the baby suckled. And when it weaned, I stopped producing.

"Mummy. Can I get another brother or a sister?" Victoria asked me some years after her little brother, Shane, was born.

"I don't think so Victoria. My eggs are done." I replied, sad that my childbearing years were over, but relieved that my monthly fertility ritual was at an end. Growing up I had wanted six children. I ended up with two of my own and a stepson — half of my wish, but 100% fulfillment with the presence of these three beautiful and amazing souls in my life.

"Why didn't you come and see me sooner?" my doctor asked me when I told her the first signs of menopause had appeared twelve months before.

"Because I was damn happy," I laughed.

Now I see my body changing in other ways, and these changes perplex me, for they seem to have no reason. Yet I know they must. The loosening and wrinkling of the skin, the achiness of bones, tightness of muscles, the movement south of tummy, breasts, butt, arms ... everything, it seems, is changing. The etches around the mouth, the dimming of eyesight, muffling of hearing, shrillness of voice. What's the meaning of all this, I wonder? The Internet, magazines, television regale me with advice on how to resist the signs of aging, how to stay firm, how to look younger, how to dress age appropriately, as if there's something wrong with all these changes that everyone who is lucky to age will experience. I try not to be offended when offered a senior citizen discount, and instead to welcome it as a manifestation of the abundance of the Universe. But I am having a hard time accepting the young man's or woman's offer of their seat on the subway. I still think I should be the one offering the seat to the elderly, and I do.

I have been wanting to get a tattoo for years. I just haven't been able to decide on where to place it. I think about how time and gravity will distort it. Do I put it on my ankle or calf where there is more bone than skin, and which therefore won't sag? Or on my back or shoulder where I won't see it anyway? Or do I get a butterfly with tiny wings on my underarm

BUTTERFLY WINGS

so that one day, I will have a grandchild in my lap, rocking, and flicking my now magnificent butterfly wings. Because, maybe, that's why everything softens.

10

LAUGHING AT THE DIRTY DISHES

Tek some, leave some.

In 2009 to 2010 when I had just moved to Toronto, I taught a course on Global Management at Ryerson University. Whilst I enjoyed sharing lessons and interacting with my students, I was drained by the time I arrived home. I would be ravenous, having not eaten since lunchtime. The thought of relaxing in my warm kitchen, doggies at my feet, happily conversing with my children, ushered me home on the cold, windy street from the Bayview subway station.

One Tuesday night, I opened my front door and headed to the kitchen to be greeted by a chaos of dishes and utensils unwashed from Sunday, floor sticky and unmopped and the garbage bin overflowing and not smelling too nice. Like a bull running in Pamplona, I charged upstairs, berating my children with each stomp of my feet, snorting venom and frustration.

"What is wrong with you children? Didn't I tell you to clean the kitchen? You each have your chores to do. Why don't you just do them?"

"I don't know why you are yelling at me," retorted Shane. "It's Vicky's turn to clean the kitchen." He stomped back into his room, slamming the door behind him. There was silence from Victoria's dark room. She was oblivious to Shane and me yelling, or she pretended to be, as there was neither movement nor sound from her teen girl haven. I collapsed onto my bed realising that the dishes would remain unwashed, unless I washed them, which I had no intention of doing.

I awoke the next morning with a stiff neck and shoulders. I crept down the stairs, to see, with no surprise, the dishes still unwashed. My body was tense and knotted and my mind equally so. I HAD to get myself out of this state – after all, isn't it I who coach clients that "for things to change you have to change?"

FORGET IT! WHAT'S THE POINT?

One by one I piled the dirty dishes and utensils into one side of the sink, determined that they would remain filthy until Victoria did her duty. But at least I could brew a cup of coffee. Comforted by my coffee, (yes, it does comfort me), I dug deep into my arsenal of state breakers and remembered that there was a Laughter Yoga session that very evening. I decided to go, even though it was all the way in Cabbage Town, a 45-minute subway ride from home. But I needed something to jerk me out of this state.

Lynn, the Laughter Yoga Leader, asked each of us to introduce ourselves by name and one thing on our minds – with laughter. The only thing on my mind was the dirty dishes. As I told the story, laughing, I realised how ridiculous the whole scene was.

"Ho-ho, ha-ha-ha!" I had spent almost 24 hours angry, frustrated, upset over dirty dishes.

"Ho-ho, ha-ha-ha!" My home was a warzone, with battle lines solidly drawn between me and my children over an unmopped floor.

"Ho-ho, ha-ha-ha!" What craziness is that? Surely if I am going to argue and fight with my children it should be about something serious?

"Ho-ho, ha-ha-ha!"

LAUGHING AT THE DIRTY DISHES

In the one hour of laughing, my body unwound, and my heart took over, moving to love rather than anger. I resolved to remain in that place, remembering that whatever the problem, whatever the question, love is the answer and that laughter is an instant shortcut. How delightful then to arrive home and find the kitchen spotlessly clean, my children calm and my home once more a sanctuary.

Of course, the story does not continue to end so happily ever after. Since then, there have been quite a few nights of dirty dishes. Now I just laugh and shift them to one side of the sink. And they get washed – not according to my schedule, but washed nonetheless. I take that back – this IS a happy ending after all, for I have been reminded of the insignificance of things and the importance of those I love. And laughter is my healer. Ho-ho! Ha-ha-ha!

11

HAPPINESS BACKLASH

Belief kill an' belief cure.

I bounded into the meeting, early as usual. "Jamaica time", which means at least half hour after the scheduled start time, was not my habit. Winston, a handsome man in the way of someone who had started work on the factory floor and had now morphed into a well-groomed business owner, was already there. For a few minutes, we engaged in the banter of those who arrive on time and who wait, as if at a government office first thing in the morning, for the clerks to appear. We were discussing the economic outlook for the nation, a negative forecast for the coming year having been released that morning. I was sharing my perspective, a positive one that focused on the silver lining. Winston barged into my sentence:

"I can't stand you people who are always happy and positive about everything. You are in denial. You need to stop it. Stop it now." He clapped his hands over his face as if there was something he just could not stomach seeing. And that was the first inkling I had that not everyone is comfortable with happiness. Winston didn't look so handsome any more.

I am a happy person. Every morning, before I peel myself out of bed, I make a conscious decision to be happy that day. I dangle my hand to the floor as a signal to the dogs that it's time to rise and shine. They gambol to my fingers, tails swishing, to sniff and lick their morning greeting. I slide out of bed, happy already that the morning has dawned with my two elderly dogs still breathing, as am I. I settle into my practice — caffeine first, always, then meditation, journaling, laughter yoga, breath of joy. The dogs, latched to my heel, trail my every move, like a chorus line of dancers. I roll out my yoga mat. Betti plops on one half. I don't have the heart to shift her. I start my sun salutations. My downward dog becomes a pyramid over her body. I focus on her instead of my navel. Then I swoop, chest suspended over her as I settle into an awkward upward facing dog. I wonder if the ancient yoga masters envisioned that the down and up dog poses could be done hovering over a dog. Her tail wags, she raises her head, our eyes meet. She's the happiest dog I have ever met, born wagging that tail. No wonder she's my favourite.

Most times my happiness routine works. But on occasion, my children will mutter about Mummy's miserableness: "What happened to free and laughing?" my daughter demands. When I am overwhelmed with a client's deadline, the stress of perfecting the report devouring my gratitude for my work, I falter. Or packing for an overseas trip, last minute anger seething, as sleep and happiness have been nowhere present in the last few days. A boyfriend breakup. A problem with money. My dogs' questioning eyes and motionless tails seem to wonder where my spirit has gone.

I think of those who have experienced horror known but unimaginable, like Alice Herz-Sommer, a Holocaust survivor. She was sent to Auschwitz as a young woman. She credited her survival to her

HAPPINESS BACKLASH

music, as she was dispatched to a special camp — a "purgatory for artists and musicians" — as her friend, a fellow musician described it. When she played, she gave hope to the other prisoners that things would get better - and hope to herself. "Every day in life is beautiful," she said in an interview when she was one hundred and four years old. "And I was always laughing — even there I was always laughing." Laughing in a concentration camp? Laughing as people were murdered all around you? Laughing at one of the darkest periods of history? Yes. For laughing keeps you in the present, keeps you from hating, frees you to hope and to love. Alice continued to laugh and play the piano until her transition five years later, the longest survivor of the Holocaust.

I once met Archbishop Desmond Tutu. He laughed the whole time. No, he didn't do laughter, he was laughter itself, happiness and joy his very being, his default state. I think about his life under apartheid in South Africa, how terrible it must have been. I think of his best friend, the Dalai Lama, who lives in exile, his life always under threat, unable to return to Tibet, his beloved home. Yet, two happier men you could never see. I keep their "Book of Joy" beside my bed, their smiling faces one of the first things I see in the morning.

Alice. The Archbishop. The Dalai Lama and many others. What am I unhappy about again? My dark moments dissipate, as certain as the night yielding to the sun.

"Happy girl," whispered my neighbour, Grace, to her elderly mother the other day as we crossed paths. I smile: Me? A girl? Happiness seems to be a most effective anti-aging serum.

"Marguerite is always smiling," mused my friend to his wife as they scanned the photographs he had taken the evening before, intrigued that one could be so all the time.

My happiness fascinates — those who are happy, for like attracts like, and those who are the opposite. The latter may declare they want to be just like me and solicit my assistance. "All who joy would win must share it. Happiness was born a twin." The words of Lord Byron, the Romantic poet, whom I studied in my high school English Literature class decades ago, spur me to help them, for to withhold would diminish my own happiness. They only want tips though, as if happiness can be lived in snippets.

And there are the happiness suckers, who, like vampires, extract the joy from others to feed their putrid lives. There are the deniers like Winston who cannot believe that happiness exists in any moment, and that it is an inner choice, irrespective of circumstances. And the saboteurs, who struggle to trip and entrap you, to grate your happiness skin until it is raw, bleeding even. They feel a moment of vindication, only a moment.

But no matter what they say or do, like Maya Angelou, another great poet "Still, I rise". Happy.

12

SMASHED AND IMPERFECT THINGS

"Cotton tree fall down, ram goat jump ovah it."

My mother's name was Daisy. She hated that name. "They named me after a cow", she used to say. Marguerite, my name, is French for Daisy. I have always loved that she named me for her in this way. I too, don't want to be named after a cow.

One Christmas, Rev. John, her dear friend and spiritual advisor, whose mother was also a Daisy, gave her a Bone China mug with daisies on it. She loved that mug. And on her passing, I captured it, seeing it as a symbol of our mother-daughter bond. It is one of the few household items I brought with me to Canada. I took special joy in sipping my first cup of coffee each morning from the daisy mug.

SMASHED AND IMPERFECT THINGS

Then one morning, just as I had brewed my coffee and had gone to my room for my quiet time, the daisy mug slipped from my hands.

"Oh no!" I exclaimed as the mug hit the ground, splinters and coffee intermingled across the floor. I looked in dismay at the pieces, remembering how Mummy used to sing "Humpty Dumpty" to us as children. Just like Humpty, I thought, all the king's horses and all the king's men, couldn't put that mug together again. "Sorry Daisy." And I laughed! For what was I apologising to Daisy for? She has no need for the mug! And really, neither do I. For what's important is not the mug, but the memories – her joy upon opening her gift from John; my pleasure in brewing her the perfect cup of coffee and serving it to her in the mug; her gratitude for the coffee, the time at my home, her quiet space. And in Canada, the memories that had continued – of opening the cupboard each morning and seeing the Daisy mug waiting to be filled; of sipping my coffee in my own quiet time; of reading and journaling with the mug by my side. I scraped up the pieces, wiped the floor and went downstairs to brew another cup of coffee.

FORGET IT! WHAT'S THE POINT?

My new handbag was perfect. It was a Christmas gift from my beloved. Walking through the Eaton Centre a few months before, I couldn't understand why he was insistent on going into the Michael Kors store. "Which do you like?" he had asked, as I ogled all the bags, mesmerised by the choices.

"This is nice." I hugged the silver tote under my arm. "But maybe the gold? What do you think?"

"So that's the one you like?"

"Yes," as I handed the bag to the salesperson, and with sadness exited the store. There was no way I would spend that amount of money for a bag when I already had more than enough in my closet.

But now, the bag was mine. The metallic gold complemented everything in my wardrobe. It was large enough to hold my MacBook Air (non-negotiable for all new handbags). The straps were long enough to fit easily under my arm, but not too long that the bag drags on the ground when I fold in my arms. There were pockets for make-up, cell phone, pens...

Pens. As instructed by the purser on the return

flight of my first trip abroad after receiving this beautiful gift, I put away everything in preparation for landing. It had turned out to be the perfect bag for travel — large enough to hold everything I needed inflight, small enough to fit beneath the seat and provide easy access to my travel necessities. I had carried it with pride and joy to my workshop in Jamaica, parading it on a table where all the ladies could see and admire it. And admire they did.

Next morning at home, I opened my bag and discovered that the gold lining was now, like a Dalmatian, littered with spots, deep blue spots. The deepest blue marked the point where the uncovered nib had drained all night. My new bag was ruined. I was upset that the bag was spoiled, even more so with myself for being so careless. But, in typical Marguerite-style, I went into fix-it mode. First stop? Google, of course. "Bag cleaning in Toronto" revealed a number of options, including one where I could get an online quote. Within 24 hours, I learned that the bag could be cleaned at an estimated cost of $104.00. Uh oh ... that's a lot of money to clean the INSIDE of a new bag.

Plan B: I checked in with the Michael Kors store

and they suggested I take it to a dry cleaner. Great — there's one right opposite my home. I dropped it off and prepared to collect it in two weeks. Alas … the dry cleaner called after a few days to advise that they could not clean it.

Plan C? I breathed. And wrote in my gratitude journal:

"I celebrate and am grateful for the blessing of my MK bag. I accept my beautiful bag as it is. It is still beautiful. It is still a beloved gift from my beloved. It is perfect."

The mug was smashed. The bag was stained. I don't even see the ink stain anymore. The love that gifted them and formed the memories has not changed. That is forever.

13

YOU DESERVE A NAME

Good fren better dan pocket money.

Jimmy, the cat at Number Eight, was getting fat. Each evening just before eight o'clock, he would stalk past my fence, paying no attention to my yapping dogs, to sit on the landing at Number Four, and wait. Jimmy's owner complained to me.

"He feeds him! I spoke to him and asked him to stop, but I don't think he has."

"Yes. I do see Jimmy sitting at his door every night. My dogs go crazy when he passes, but he doesn't pay them any mind. He's on a mission," I chuckled.

"I wish he wouldn't do it. You know cats. No matter what I do, Jimmy goes over there. If you see him passing your house, please chase him back over."

I promise to do so. But sure enough, as I journey past Number Four the next night, there is Jimmy, eyes fixated on the morsels cascading from the man's hands to be caught in his grateful jaws just before hitting the concrete floor.

"You are feeding the cat," I call out, masquerading my accusation as a casual observation, thinking to make peace between my neighbours.

"Yes," he replies, continuing to drop the food for Jimmy to devour. "But he asks me," he adds with a shrug when I point out how plump Jimmy is getting. And so, Jimmy gets fatter.

"You work too hard," he would say as I trudged past his house, laden with groceries from Loblaw's across the street, just before their 11.00 p.m. closing. He would be there, no matter the season or the weather, front door ajar, standing still, smoking, pensive, but always acknowledging my presence.

"Where are your children? Why don't they help you?" He reads my mind. I try to wave, but the bags are too heavy, instead replying with a nod, disconcerted that he thinks I am spoiling my children.

YOU DESERVE A NAME

A wall about four feet high, low enough for even me to see over, but adequate to give us both privacy, separates our tiny yards. Mine: a summer cornucopia of tomatoes, sweet peppers, lettuce, strawberries, basil, thyme, lemongrass and even a grapevine that I coax to remain on my side. His: two red plastic Adirondack chairs tucked behind three bushes, no fence, just the little hedge and a lawn, always lush and green after the spring thaw, despite his inattention. In earlier years, every morning of spring and summer, he would place a birdcage on the patio. I would hear the happy chirps of two budgies from my bedroom on the second floor. Caged, yet, like us humans, I would think, they revel in the freedom from winter, the cold, the isolation, the dreariness.

"You are gardening today," he would observe, cigarette between the second and third digits of his right hand as he leaned against his doorway, shifting from one foot to the other until the cigarette died.

"I'm trying kale this year. And the strawberries I planted last year are coming up again," I would banter, coffee mug in one hand, hose in the other, urging my plants to bear before the end of summer. He would nod, smiling. I remembered my sister remarking that if only he didn't smoke, he might be a good match for me.

But one morning, as I was being tugged out the yard by my dogs for their walk to the park, I found him agitated, distressed eyes peeled to the sky.

"My daughter's bird has escaped. He won't come back. She's away. How am I going to tell her when she comes home tomorrow?" He groaned, hands clutched to his temple, as he pleaded with his entire being for the return of the bird, now perched in sweet liberation on the edge of the roof. I stood with him in parental solidarity until my dogs outlived their patient sitting and tugged on their leashes. How does one break bad news to one's child? Days later, I enquired if the bird had returned. "No," the despondence of his reply belying his skyward gaze.

"I rescued your dogs," he reported one time on my return from a business trip abroad, as I walked past his home from my foray to Loblaw's.

"I saw them running past my house, so I chased them back and put them in your yard. Your door was open, but I didn't see anyone. I called, and your son answered from inside. Your children didn't tell you?"

Of course, my children hadn't told me. They, like

my dogs, thought their secret was safe with him. But it was not: parental solidarity has no secrets. We protect each other to protect our children, to make sure that they do the right thing. That's what he brought from his home country. I understood, as in Jamaica we do the same. In Canada, political correctness says to mind our own business. I thanked him. Anyone who rescues my dogs is my hero.

Some afternoons I glimpsed him walking past my house, a worn LCBO plastic reusable bag clutched to his heart, gaze steadfast on his mission. Later, I would see him on the patio, his greying, balding dome just visible above the hedge. A slight whiff of alcohol. He would sit until darkness enveloped the evening, the red tip of his cigarette the only evidence of his presence.

I saw him happy once. We met on the path outside our homes with my sister and the dogs. His face was bronze from the sun, but more so from joy that stretched his smile into a bowl-like crescent from ear to ear. His eyes twinkled with happiness.

"I went home to Romania," he informed before I could even ask, "I was there for three weeks."

And I realised that the Romania that was his home

was not the Romania I had envisaged from media reports — Ceaușescu's brutality, deprivation and austerity, starving orphans begging to be adopted by kind, desperate Americans. The Romania that was his home, that made him glow, was family, memories, love. Like all of us, no matter how terrible it may seem to others, home is home.

Six autumns. Six winters. Six springs. But only five summers.

One afternoon as I neared home, a woman who looked to be in her forties, whom I didn't recognise, but who seemed familiar, emerged from his house. A policeman was seated in one of his red plastic Adirondack chairs.

"Did something happen?" I asked.

"Yes, something happened," the woman responded as she stomped past me, head down, trying to hide the tears staining her face.

"The gentleman passed," said the policeman, his face sombre from too many occasions of delivering such news, but kind nonetheless.

I paid my final respects through the blinds of my bedroom window as the black shrouded stretcher was wheeled past my home. There were so many questions I wanted to ask. What did you do for a living? When did you come to Canada? What was it like growing up in Romania? How many siblings did you have? Are your parents still alive? But mostly, what is your name?

14

FROM HOME

Learn fi dance a yard before yuh dance abroad.

Canada is the surprise that my fifties brought me. It was as much a part of my life plan as a moon odyssey.

In the summer of my eighth year, I boarded a plane for the first time. My mother, her eldest sibling, Winnie, and my five-year old sister, Carole, journeyed to Denver, Colorado to visit my mother's other sister, Perle. Perle, her husband Hugh and their four children had migrated from Jamaica to Denver in the 1950s for my uncle to assume a position as minister of a Presbyterian church. Carole and I were dolled up, for one dressed for travel in those days. We had matching bags, mine red, Carole's green,

FROM HOME

stuffed with the necessities of children's travel — books, crayons, Barbie dolls. Denver was the first leg on our transcontinental expedition. There were church picnics and parties where we marvelled at children speaking "American"; a foray to a national park dotted with patches of snow, even in summer, and a roadside stop where Carole and I posed on a stuffed buffalo beside a feathered head-dressed chief, cowboy and Indian movies that we had watched in Jamaica brought to life. Laughter sewed together the distance of time and geography endured by Perle and her sisters, Carole and I absorbing these moments that would embroider our own tapestry of sisterhood in years to come.

A week later, we embarked for Toronto to visit my mother's school friend, Gertie. The Greyhound bus took three days. There was no toilet on the bus, so we had to "hold it" until we arrived at the stations that were strung like beads on a necklace of highways from Colorado through Kansas, Missouri, Illinois, Indiana, Michigan and across the border to Canada. We disembarked in Toronto, where the locals told us it was warm, it being summer, but chilly and grey to this little tropical bird. Toronto in 1964: Casa Loma, real Christmas trees in front yards, squirrels, are all I remember. And greyness.

In April 1975, a gaggle of student athletes, musicians, singers and dancers from the University of the West Indies Mona Campus flew through the night from Jamaica to Trinidad to the annual Intercampus Games and Arts Festival. I was a member of the Mona Dance Troupe and this was my first visit to Trinidad. The sun had started to emerge from the east of the mountains of the Northern Range that crested the St. Augustine campus; wild parrots and kiskidees competed to out-screech the other; pink and yellow cotton candy flowers burst from the poui, guango and cassia trees dotting the campus. How grey all the buildings are, I thought, as we disembarked the bus in the parking lot at Canada Hall, one of the student halls of residence. Aptly named, I further mused, recalling that grey childhood summer in Toronto, black and white photographs of the Canadian Shield in high school Geography books, and of the Arctic tundra in the Life and National Geographic magazines to which my father subscribed as our window to the world outside our small island home.

FROM HOME

My Canadian friends in the Class of 1985 at Harvard Business School looked to their grand southern neighbour for their future, their MBAs VIP tickets. Like them, I had no desire to live in Canada, nor to remain in America, as they did. Indeed, so certain was I that my life of building, contributing to and living in Jamaica was my destiny, that whilst my classmates interviewed for jobs, I was taking pottery and tap dance classes in Harvard Square. Within weeks of graduation, I was back "on the rock" as we Jamaicans refer to our island, certain that this was where I would grow old and die.

Two decades later, I had had enough of Jamaica.

Enough of witnessing young Jamaican athletes at our High School Athletic Championships, running to escape poverty, but finding that they could not outrun it. The river of talent never abates — like the hatching of turtles on shores around the Caribbean, their chances of survival minimal, it happens every year. Hope is a powerful thing.

Enough of hearing "crats" — technocrats, bureaucrats — opine: "Well you know . . . Some good things are happening" at meetings, conferences, workshops, seminars where we "plan" for the future, on a garbage heap of excuses. I wondered how they could not see that those "good things" are aberrations, not the norm, infinitesimal in the sea of possibilities. I wondered what part I had played in it.

Enough of insulating my children from Jamaican life, trying to recreate for them the freedom of my childhood. My gang of friends and cousins walked the streets and trekked the gullies and expanse of the Knutsford Park, a former racehorse track, dotted with wild, prickled macca brush and coolie plum trees. As we grew into adulthood, it had morphed into the vibrant commercial centre of New Kingston. Girls we were, roaming free around Kingston without fear, without incident. My children roamed free in our fenced yard.

Enough of the five-year olds trekking down Norbrook Drive in the pre-dawn darkness past my 5.00 a.m. running group. "Mawnin' Miss," they would proffer, with smiles that made you think the sun had already risen. So neat these children were, the girls in navy blue uniforms starched crisp like fried green plantain, red bows and clips adorning their hair like ladybugs, the boys in khaki pants and shirts that threatened to out-crisp the girls' uniforms. They walked miles to school, the schools that would fail most of them, graduating many barely literate, but with a certificate, cap and gown, loosing them onto society, ill-prepared for the economic needs of the 21st century. A society that would then turn their backs and say, "What is wrong with the young people of today? They have no ambition, no manners, no values."

Enough of the place that is my home. Brazil, South Africa, Japan, Hong Kong, Germany, America, Harvard — no matter where I travelled there would be a conversation like this:

"Where are you from?"

"Jamaica"

"Ah, Jamaica!" paradise lighting their faces as they went to the secret nirvana in their soul that is Jamaica. Jamaica, the place of magic that hands the world its most precious gifts — Marcus Garvey, Bob Marley, Mary Seacole, Usain Bolt, Michael Manley, Louise Bennett — a few of the never-ending river of brilliance, excellence and light. Yet, Jamaica does not nurture, and so many Jamaicans succeed in spite of, not because of.

FORGET IT! WHAT'S THE POINT?

Those two decades between business school and "enough" were the busiest of my life. There were the typical life transitions: marriage, stepmothering, babies, separation, divorce, single motherhood. I left corporate life and started businesses. I served on corporate boards, volunteered in trade associations, committees and for causes. I tried to give my children a world view – travel overseas and around Jamaica, the theatre and of course, *National Geographic* magazines.

I created a haven in my home. The trampoline on our front lawn had my children and their friends leaping, tumbling, laughing for hours into the night. Mango, avocado, ackee, breadfruit, guava, soursop, lime, grapefruit and otaheite apple trees in our yard rained fruit on us throughout the year. My children climbed trees and ate tree-ripened, just-picked mangoes and apples, spread-eagled on the ground or straddled over branches of the fruit-heavy trees. And my massive ferns, orbs that stretched to the roof and grazed the ground, swung from the front porch, like the gardens in ancient Babylon, nestling my meditation nook. There were birthday parties with donkey carts, clowns, storytellers and bounceabouts; Christmas carol sing-alongs, and one grand fete with over 300 of my closest friends, to herald my fiftieth birthday.

"You know, Mummy, we really had a happy childhood. Didn't we Shane?" my daughter Victoria said one Sunday morning, as we loitered over breakfast.

"Uh-huh," her brother Shane nodded and grunted.

But there came a time when Jamaica was not enough for me. In August 2009, I sold or gave away almost everything I owned, my precious books last, and packed my two children, three dogs and a few suitcases of personal belongings for Canada.

Now, my mind wanders south from this new country, where I have learned that the sunniest days are the coldest, where lips remind me of creases in the crisp khaki pants of little Jamaican boys rather than of their sunshine smiles; where the children I pass on my morning runs bow their heads and look away, trying hard not to make eye contact, with never a "Mawnin' Miss"; where reserved, polite people speak in low tones, contrast to the Jamaican raucousness, colour and chaos. I miss the energy of Jamaica, even whilst appreciating the order of Canada. Must be old age, I muse.

FORGET IT! WHAT'S THE POINT?

A year after my migration to Canada, I returned home to Jamaica on my third trip since leaving. I had a strange feeling of detachment as the plane landed at the Norman Manley International Airport in Kingston, and as I drove through the streets of the city to my brother's home. I passed by my old residence where I had lived for 16 years, where my children and numerous litters of puppies were born and raised, where I planted trees and tended a garden, celebrated birthdays, Christmas and other special and not-so-special occasions, and had worked from my home office. It was no longer my mine, despite the millions of memories.

Was I now a visitor to Jamaica, my home?

15

THE DAY CAN WAIT

De only ting for me,
Is mi bowl a bwiling coffee in di mawnin.

In the pre-caffeine dawn, I stumble down the stairs to my kitchen, coffee anticipation luring me forward. Both sides of the sink are packed higher than last night, plates, pots, knives, forks, spatula, spoons, the detritus of my children turning night into day, the pasta-caked pot and chicken-greased frying pan, evidence of cooking at some unknown nocturnal hour.

I rummage for the stainless-steel milk jug beneath the tumble of mess in the sink, wondering why I didn't wash it immediately I used it yesterday morning. Eking space between the dirty dishes and the tap, I scrub the cement of yesterday's milk. With a flick of my wrist, I dash cold half and half organic milk about 1/3rd to the rim and place it on the small rear stove burner, on high. I stretch to the cupboard above my head for the organic Fair Trade dark roast coffee beans that, according to the label, promise "citrus notes, wood smoke & a dark chocolate finish".

The rice cooker, still on warm from last night, camouflages the coffee grinder. Shane loves rice, no matter the hour. Two scoops of coffee beans, ground until fine. Cold water — half the manufacturers' recommended amount: my coffee must be doubly strong. I smile as I remember my best friend, June, who introduced me to coffee and who passed away twenty three years before: "I like my coffee like my men, black and strong." I still hear her sweet giggle as she said that, recalling many mornings at her breakfast table, cups warming our hands as we chatted about coffee and men, both of various strength and hues. I miss her.

The grinding sound travels up to my bedroom, to awaken the dogs. The clink of the City of Toronto and rabies licences, chorused with soft pads down

THE DAY CAN WAIT

the stairs, heralds Itsy, the first as always to appear. I sneak her a treat, succumbing to her pleading eyes. I hear the heavier pad and slower tag clink of Betti labouring down, her ever-wagging tail pleading like Itsy's eyes for her treat. I shovel the coffee grounds into the filter holder, careful to wipe the rim clean, as my brother always reminds me when I visit his home in Jamaica, so that there is no escape for the steam, save pressured down through the dark fine grounds. The carafe that came with the machine broke long ago so I place the blue cup with the Mickey Mouse handle beneath the filter holder. This was my gift to Mummy when I ran the Disney marathon. Now it's mine. And I remember how much she used to enjoy my coffee.

The milk boils up and overflows. I snap off the dial on the stove, then grab the hand-held frother from behind the jungle of appliance wires. Drat. It needs batteries. Four new batteries lodged in place, the frother urges the hot milk ever higher up the stainless-steel jug. The brew spews from the brew head, slows to a trickle, then a drip, then nothing. Like a waterfall cascading through a narrow crack in a ravine, I pour the cloud of milk into the half-filled mug of mud-like espresso and gently stir it, wondering how baristas create those cute little heart shapes.

I sit on the bottom rung of the stepladder in the corner, cup warming my palms. The dogs lurch forward to nest at my feet. The warm, dark liquid flits across the tip of my tongue and leaves a shock of comfort, bitterness and chocolate. I am surprised – chocolate? Hot. That first sip tells me. Sip slowly. With a second clip of the coffee, the mug snuggled between my hands, I feel the warmth of the liquid and of deep memories.

Memories of coffee and good times – June, Mummy, a family reunion in Costa Rica, at my cousin Odel's house in Limon, a bundle of family tumbling in from a day exploring our family history. Brewing coffee in the sock. The sock! Memories of roly-poly Auntie Perle, my mother's sister who lived in Denver and then Los Angeles, demonstrating with an outrageous chuckle how magnificently the sock drips coffee – and how cheap it is, she marvelled, again with a chuckle. Memories of coffee and routine – Daddy's daily habit of lunch, coffee and a nap, the Latin siesta hinting at vestiges of our family ancestry shining through generations later in his daily respite. Memories of coffee and my business in Jamaica — the offering to whomever came through the door — Milverton, our client; Mr. Hill, our landlord; Norman, our neighbour — each loving the love expressed in the coffee.

My third sip reaches further back on my tongue to rest in the middle, in the slight indentation that causes a pause. Full flavour bursts forth — surprise! It's not so bitter after all. I allow it to slide out of the indentation to the back of my tongue, down my throat, already anticipating the fourth sip. More like a gulp now that the liquid has cooled to a comfortable feel: equilibrium — warm enough to be comforting, but not too warm to be uncomfortable.

Betti shifts from side to side to keep her paws from splaying on the tile floor. Itsy stretches into an upward facing dog yoga asana. So that's how it's supposed to look, I think, now understanding what my yoga teacher, Donovan, has been trying to tell me for years. Itsy nudges my elbow, Betti digs her snout into my groin. Time to get going they seem to be saying. The day awaits. But the day can wait.

16

MISS CHIN PICKS UP THE POOP

Tek bad sinting mek laugh.

I couldn't believe it. Did I actually see the woman, through the slats in the fence, dash a black and white polka-dotted bag of dog poop behind the tree?

I leaned forward from the teak chaise where I had been reading, my dogs, Betti and Itsy, nestled in my lap. The poop-dropping woman by now had spun, chin length bob swinging, her sweatshirt a cardinal blur, hastening away down the path. Her brindle-coloured dog strained at the leash, pulling her on, his duty now done.

"Excuse me miss," I ventured with hesitation still not believing what I had just witnessed.

MISS CHIN PICKS UP THE POOP

"Hello," raising my voice as the red sweatshirt and dog receded further from view, clapping my hands yet conscious of not disturbing the quietude of the early weekend morning. "Please pick up after your dog, madam."

The woman's head turned as her gait slowed. I didn't know her or her name, but I recognised the dog. Always thought he was an odd, ugly creature — brindle body, solid brown head. In Jamaica, she would be known as "Miss Chin", which is what they call every woman of Chinese ethnicity down there. Miss Chin, in my mind, how could you do such a nasty thing? Now people will think I'm the nasty one, as you have dropped the bags right outside my home. Some people really shouldn't live with other people.

Walking towards her I notice behind the tree, not one, but four black and white polka-dotted poop bags, one burst open, blackened with flies. I don't believe it! She has been doing this all along. And imagine, just last week I had congratulated and thanked the property managers for placing poop bins throughout the compound. What's wrong with this woman? Miss Chin stands alert. Her jaw slack, mouth open, she glares at me, upset that she has been called out. Her dog continues to pull on the leash.

"There is a poop bin around the corner. Could you please pick up your bags and dispose of them there? This is right outside my home and it attracts flies."

"I didn't drop those."

"But you did. I saw you."

"Are you accusing me?"

It's now my turn to glare. Yes, Miss Chin, I mutter to myself. I saw you. If only my dogs could speak, they saw you too! They even leaped off the chaise and ran to the gate. Maybe they couldn't believe your nastiness too.

"Lady," thinking that she is anything but, "I saw when you threw the bag behind the tree. I was sitting right there," pointing to my patio.

Miss Chin's eyes widened, opening now to the fact there was a witness to her furtive deed. "I can't pick it up now. I don't have any bags."

Ah! I win. She's acknowledging her wrongdoing and going to make amends. "I have bags inside. Hold on and I will get some for you."

Pivoting, I open my gate and stride up the path

towards my front door to get the bags. I glimpse a flash of red disappearing at the periphery of my sight, as a black and white polka dotted poop bag plops three inches from my heel.

A few days later as I am walking my dogs, Miss Chin approaches. She smiles; I glare; she says hello. In shock, I mumble a return greeting, and then smile, noticing my dogs' wagging tails as they strain to sniff her dog. We continue on our separate ways. Nearing my gate, I glance to my left – the bags of poop behind the tree are gone. How quickly we forget.

17

TO HOME

New broom sweep clean but ol' broom know di corner.

On December 13, 2013, I took my oath of citizenship. I was now a Canadian.

I had received the call for the citizenship ceremony at very short notice. I had booked to go to New York to see my friend's daughter perform in "The Nutcracker". I was to have departed on the Friday evening and thought I could make it in time from the citizenship ceremony. Then I found out that I had to surrender my Permanent Resident card before the ceremony. Until I applied for and got my Canadian passport, I was a prisoner in Canada. I could not leave. Or rather, I could, but I would have no papers

To Home

to return. I cancelled my trip. And the weekend was open. Nothing to do on that weekend. Except to relive the ceremony.

I had a meeting the morning of the ceremony, north of Toronto. My clients, a group of Canadian CEOs, were thrilled. Their faces beamed their love and congratulations as they bid me farewell, and welcomed me to becoming one of them, a Canadian citizen. My son, Shane, who was also being inducted, met me at the Immigration Office. We surrendered our Permanent Residency cards. I felt vulnerable watching the officer drop them into a box at her feet, realising that until I received my Certificate of Citizenship, I had no status. We sat in the third row of a large hall with "True North Strong and Free" emblazoned on the wall. The Canadian flag stood guard at the judge's bench. I looked around, noticing the human bouquet of all ages, ethnicities, colour, dress and languages, about to become citizens. "Yes. This is Canada," I mused. A charming gentleman with an open, glowing face and a Broadway musical voice approached the lectern and called the proceedings to order. The judge entered. He welcomed us with the tale of his own experience as an immigrant, what it meant to him to become a citizen and what our responsibilities as new citizens would be. We recited the Oath of Citizenship, citizenship officers policing the group to make sure everyone uttered the words. Then, one by one, we were called to receive our Certificate. The judge understood our joy and was happy to pose for photographs with each new citizen. The final name called, we rose and sang the Canadian National Anthem. I cried.

"So sistah, do you feel any different?" my brother-in-law, Arsenio, asked me the next day, as I entered his kitchen. I peeled off my winter coat and seated myself at the kitchen table. He turned the chicken in the frying pan, lifting each piece with the tenderness of someone who loves to cook. He does. He has dreams of one day becoming a chef in Canada. Originally from Cuba, Arsenio moved to Jamaica to dance in the national company, where he met my sister, also a dancer. Their move to Canada was the second major relocation in his life. He had adjusted to being a Jamaican; now he was curious about becoming a Canadian.

Did I feel any different? I had gone to bed as usual the previous night, the magazine I was

To Home

reading slipping from my hands as my body sank into the sweet release of sleep. Did I feel any different this Saturday morning as I wandered through my "hello day" ritual — grinding coffee beans, brewing coffee, frothing the cream, letting out the doggies, rubbing their sweet bellies on their return and resisting their entreating eyes to give them more treats?

Yes, I did feel different. It was a gentle type of feeling, yet intense at the same time, a tumble of emotions at the culmination of a long-awaited and much anticipated outcome; the emotions one feels when you finally get that something that you have held firm in your sight. What changed?

I was the same Marguerite — weighed the same, lived in the same home, the same three dogs resting at my feet, the same two children snug asleep in their beds on the snowy Canadian winter morning. I had the same list of things-to-do awaiting Monday — complete a report for my client, finish (more like start) my Christmas shopping, get my nails done, go to the grocery — the same details that permeated my life from day to day. Yet, I did feel different. I chuckled as I nursed a second cup of coffee in Arsenio's kitchen, sharing the details of the ceremony, responding to his questions. Underlying our banter was this thought: the oath of citizenship is like a marriage, and the ceremony yesterday was the wedding. Permanent residency was shacking up, testing the waters of compatibility. Citizenship is permanent. It is a mutual commitment to a country and the country to you. And I plan on never getting a divorce.

But what about Jamaica, the beloved land of my birth, my native land: the repository of infinite memories, bitter, sweet and the full range in between; the stirrer of my emotions — intense love for the beauty of the land and the magnificent, vibrant energy of my people, as well as frustration, worry, guilt and anger at the betrayal of hope. Do I now love thee less, Jamaica? Are you no longer home?

What is this thing we called home, I pondered, donning my coat and boots to return to my apartment. It's a physical place, where one is born and lives. It's a country, a city, a building. We have many such places in our lifetime, most of which we call home. But the home for which we yearn, the deepest yearning of our heart is a place where we feel safe, accepted and understood, where we find peace

TO HOME

and happiness. It is the place where we exhale deeply. It is an inner place.

"I long, as does every human being, to be at home wherever I find myself," wrote Maya Angelou. When home is this place, independent of physical matter, we are truly home. This is when we realise that home is love. When my daughter, Victoria, was born in 1993, I felt an intense swelling of primal love that I could not ever have imagined. Two years later when my son, Shane, was born, I was a bit worried that I would have to divide this love, to love Victoria less in order to hold Shane in my heart. Instead, my love expanded exponentially to hold them both always and forever. The lesson: there is no limit to love. Love cannot be divided, it can only expand. Love is what makes home be wherever I am. Love is what makes me not have to choose between Jamaica and Canada.

Now, when I awaken in the Blue Mountains on my visits home to Jamaica, my heart pulses with a line from a song we learned at school:

"I saw my land in the morning, and
Oh, but she was fair."
(Words by M.G. Smith; Music by Mapletoft Poulle)

And when I run in the mornings in the Toronto ravines, my heart likewise sings.

Oh, Canada. I am committed to you. You may not be my native land, but you are my home.

Ah, Jamaica. I am committed to you. You are my native land, and always my home.

18

FROM BAY STREET TO BAYVIEW

A pound ah fret cyaan pay an ounce ah debt.

"Then, why don't you just get a job?" my daughter Victoria shouted. "I just don't understand why you can't get a job. I am tired of you telling us you don't have any money." She charged up the stairs to her bedroom and slammed the door.

Her words weighed heavy, bringing my head to rest on the kitchen counter, as tough and immovable as the despair I felt.

Eight months before, I had moved with my two teenagers from Jamaica to Toronto, accompanied, like all immigrants, with our invisible hope and dreams. Our life had been good in Jamaica. But it was going to be even better in Canada.

The children were now settled into high school. In Jamaica, they had worn regulation uniforms; in Toronto, the standard was whatever they rolled out of bed into that morning. They were horrified that the students didn't stop talking when the teacher entered the classroom, and they loved walking or taking the subway to school rather than being chauffeured by me. It was so North America, just like the schools they used to watch on American sitcoms on television in Jamaica. Plus, the coolness of being Jamaican and of being friends with one of Bob Marley's granddaughters conferred celebrity status at school. They were happy.

Job One done, I turned to my own welfare, absorbed with ad hoc projects and teaching global business part time at Ryerson University. I knew that opportunities would emerge, just as surely as the trees bud and blossom after the long, cold winter. After all, I had come to Canada armed with a Harvard MBA, certification and considerable experience as a coach and facilitator, numerous years in consulting, including for the Canadian government and Canadian consulting firms and decades of starting and running businesses. Even I was impressed with my resume.

But I was getting desperate. My resources were dwindling and "We don't have the money," had become a daily refrain. In my entire career, I had only been employed by someone else for 3½ years. Since 1990, I employed myself. But, this is Canada. And I needed to be open to new things. Thus commenced my job hunt odyssey.

I did everything I was told to do – I reworked and revised my resume to get it to the recommended two pages, eliminating anything that would imply my age, which also meant deleting much of my experience. I masked that all of my working experience was outside of Canada, since I was told that Canadian experience was paramount. I applied for jobs online, crafting my cover letters for the nuances of each job. I networked incessantly, trotting downtown for 7.00 a.m. breakfasts to share with other desperate seekers the wonders of me. And I pulled strings, getting access to a few C-suites.

Yet, all this did not seem to mean anything to the

bottomless File 13 hole that my applications seemed to fall into. There was no job offer.

I sank deeper and deeper into despair, as I pillaged my savings. I started to doubt myself and all that I had achieved. "Was it because I was black, a woman, too old, have an accent or, God forbid, laugh too much?" I asked myself. Friends and acquaintances suggested desperate measures: "Take Harvard off your resume". "Cut your locks to look more corporate." I lodged those in the crevices of my desperation, hoping that I would never have to dig that deep.

One thing that kept me going was my daily walks with my three doggies. I would leash them up and we would strike out for the park, no matter how unhappy I was feeling. Nothing like having to scoop poop three times per day for three dogs to let you know you have a purpose. And as I walked behind their pert, wagging tails, I would sing my favourite Bob Marley song: *"Don't worry 'bout a thing, 'cause every little thing gonna be alright".* But on other days, the really dark ones, I would curl up in bed under the comforter and cry for my mummy. I just wanted her comfort and love, to remind me of who I am and how precious and valuable I am to this world.

Then, on October 27, 2010, I was in an interview at one of the big banks on Bay Street. This was the third position I was interviewing for here. The talent managers loved me and were determined to find a place for me. I was sitting in front of a department head, telling her about a time when, and another time when, all of a sudden, I witnessed myself from outside of my body. I realised that I did not want this job, I did not want to work for this woman, I did not want to work for this organisation. Yet, if she offered me the job, the Marguerite sitting in the chair would take it. But my desperation had reached its limit and, like an elastic band stretched too far, something within me snapped.

I thanked her for her time, not caring if I ever heard from her again, discarding my despair in her office on the 10th floor. As the elevator descended, my joy ascended. I pranced through the underground corridor to the subway and danced into the waiting carriage. I looked around at the mass of moribund commuters, the stress of their daily 9 to 5 creasing their foreheads, happy now that I had released myself from a similar fate. On the ride from Bay Street to the Bayview Station, I decided: to hell with asking and begging people for a job; I was going to do what I had always done – make my own. Within that 45-minute subway ride, I abandoned my job search.

That night, I went online and registered my own business. I spent the next day out with friends, as I no longer had the daily grind of trolling job boards and sending out resumes. On my return home that evening, I logged into Gmail to find this message from a former client:

"Marguerite. Are you available to come to Jamaica in January to do a strategy retreat?"

Later that evening, as we set the table for dinner, I said to Victoria:

"Guess what? I got a job!"

19

A Cloud of Love

Every dog 'ave 'im day, an' every puss, 'im 4 o'clock.

What goes through a dog's mind? Do they have conscious thoughts? I have "owned" many dogs throughout my life. But one, Cloud, a Shih Tzu poodle mix, was my companion through the most challenging and transformative period of my life — single motherhood. On dark days, I would hug her and gaze into her eyes, imagining her story, from her point of view.

I remember the day when, as a six-week old puppy, a lady and her two children arrived. They stooped to caress me, their happy cries stinging my tiny ears. I shrank to the rear of the den, trembling. I didn't know what was happening. I loved my fluffy mother, her warm, cosy body, and her sweet always-available milk. But lately, I had noticed when we suckled, she snapped at my brothers and me and skittered away like the lizards we chased. Was it time for us to leave her? The little girl, Victoria, I heard them call her, trundled me into her arms, pivoted and walked away. I never saw my mother or brothers again.

Do dogs understand concepts, like family?

"She reminds me of a fluffy cloud," the mommy murmured. Cloud. That was my name. And the mommy, Victoria and her brother, Shane, were now my humans. They giggled when I wagged my tail. I wiggled and gurgled when they rubbed my tummy. I was hardly ever allowed on the ground. They passed me from one embrace to the other. I learned to snuggle into the crevices of their bodies, keeping warm and remembering what my real mother felt like. They got excited when I yawned. One would hoist me, noses would jostle for space in my open snout, sighs of satisfaction exhaling at the smell of my breath. Even the mommy did it. It seemed to give them great pleasure. They kept saying it's the sweetest smell in the world. Humans are weird. But I loved making them happy.

Do dogs know emotions? Do they consciously choose them?

A CLOUD OF LOVE

Victoria and Shane grew, and so did I. I whiled away my days exploring the yard, chewing on the mangoes fallen beneath the trees, chasing lizards and mice and trying to get Minnie, the old Rottweiler, to play. I especially loved when mommy and I fetched Victoria and Shane from school. I missed them so much when they left each morning. How I wagged my little body and licked their faces when they jumped into the car! Home we went for play, cuddles and then sweet sleep in their arms.

I had two litters of puppies. My first litter was eight, but my first born, a big black and white boy, died. That left Betti, my brown baby, as my favourite. All the humans adored her because she was ever happy, wagging her tail before she could even toddle. I was thrilled when mommy decided to keep her. I loved my humans, but I longed for some doggie company. Two years later, I produced a second litter. That didn't go so well. There were seven pups and two died at birth. I ignored the tiniest one, giving my all to the healthy pups, but the mommy kept force-feeding her on my teats. That was uncomfortable. But the puppy survived. The mommy said she couldn't send her away, having saved her life, so Itsy stayed with us.

Betti, Itsy and I spent many happy years with our people. Each morning as mommy savoured her coffee in the garden, I traced the perimeter of the yard, sniffing the new day. I had a routine: check in with the big outside dogs, Minnie, Mooshie and Mufasa: note fruit that had fallen overnight, probe any newly-dead mice, lizards or frogs, then race in to awaken the children. Alarm clock duty completed, I lay on the patio with the other five dogs, the Jamaican morning sunshine cuddling us with its warmth. Once the children left for school, the silence of the house embraced us, and we napped on mommy's couch while she worked, every now and then raising our heads to make sure she was still there. In the afternoons, when it was nearing the time for the children to return, we squeezed through the front door grilles, trotted up the driveway and pressed our noses to the gate, wondering if each approaching car would be the one to bring them home. As they grew, Victoria and Shane spent less time at home, running in and out with their friends, trailing quick goodbyes and fleeting kisses. But we waited, tails ready to wag whenever they returned.

Betti and Itsy each bore a litter of puppies. Purlie, one of Itsy's puppies stayed with us. She was a happy, energetic one. The mommy would sometimes laugh and say, "Purlie. You are not coming with us to Canada. You are too wild." One morning, we saw her in a box, lying still while the mommy, Victoria and Shane sobbed. They said she ran out on the street the night before and a car hit her. We had wondered where she was last night, but figured she was curled up in one of the children's beds. We sniffed her body and ran off. We knew she had gone, and would not be coming with us to Canada, wherever that was. But why were the humans so sad?

Do dogs know death?

Our pack of dogs grew when Daisy, a rambunctious mongrel arrived. I didn't like her too much as she harassed me whenever I went outside. Minnie died, as did Mooshie, the other Rottweiler. Our human grandmother, Daisy, also passed away. We missed her because she brought us bones and treats when she visited and made sure to pat each of us. Betti would try to jump in her lap as she sat in the rocking chair. "Get down, Betti," she would say. I think she liked Itsy the best, as she was allowed to cuddle in her lap.

And then we noticed that our people were clearing out the house. Furniture disappeared. People arrived and removed boxes. I liked that, because sometimes when things were moved, lizards jumped out and I got to chase them. Then one day, our humans disappeared. We were accustomed to them leaving, but this time was different. We sensed it in their tears. That was the worst day of my life. I didn't know what was going on. Where had they gone? Why did they leave us? Would we ever see them again? We huddled together, three balls of fear in the housekeeper's room, or waiting at the gate, seeking solace and comfort from each other. A few days later, Auntie Carole, mommy's sister, took us away from our home. This was the only home Betti and Itsy had ever known: the place where we all had puppies, romped in the yard with our people and their friends, and snoozed on the back patio. Auntie Carole took us to a kennel where there were lots of other dogs. Strange humans cared for us. For the first time in our lives, we were put in cages. We made friends, but mostly we stuck together. We were a pack. But where were our humans?

Then one morning, I almost jumped out of my fluffy white coat with joy. My mommy was back! Oh, how happy I was to see her. I crawled into the crook of her neck and clung to her, hoping she would never leave us again. But she did. Would I ever see her, Victoria and Shane, my own human children, again? A few days later, she returned with Auntie Carole and her son, Kyle. This time they put us in their car and drove away. I yapped in my doggie language: "We're going home."

A CLOUD OF LOVE

Do dogs have language? What do their sounds mean?

But we weren't. They took us to a building, bigger than our home, and placed us in cages again — Betti in one and Itsy and me in the other. As the gates closed, we heard our mommy whisper, "Bye babies! See you soon." A man in a uniform loaded our cages on a trolley and took us away. We trembled and tried to steady ourselves as the cages were rolled out and then into a huge, light blue contraption with a large red maple leaf painted on the side.

What do dogs see? Can they distinguish shapes? Do dogs recognise colour?

The door closed. It was dark and cold. Had we died? Loud noises bombarded our ears; the contraption rattled. Itsy shook beside me. Our ears hurt. We whimpered, letting each other know that we were there for each other. At last the door peeled open to a sky laden with grey. Strange looking humans lifted our cages and rolled us along to another large cavern. We were happy to be out of the darkness, but we felt so cold. Where was this place? Could this be doggie heaven? We soon found out that it was, when our mommy appeared. I was so happy I couldn't stop barking. Later, I heard her telling people that the whole of Pearson Airport heard me. Once again, mommy put us in a car, still in our cages. Even though she was with us, I continued to yap my confusion. Where were we? Where was she taking us? The car halted. The driver raised the rear door and there were Victoria and Shane greeting us with squeals, hugs and kisses. We knew then that we were home.

My days passed in this new place in slumber with brief forays outside. Each morning as mommy opened the front door, I trundled down the stairs to sniff the new day. I wasn't seeing or hearing too well. The front door opening sometimes heralded a surprise — a blanket of white, or orange and brown, sometimes shades of pink and green or bright colour, like the home we knew in Jamaica. I would trace the perimeter of the little yard. I missed chasing lizards, which were easier to catch than the squirrels here. Betti, Itsy and I still waited by the door for our humans, joyful as ever to see them at the close of each day. For all that had changed, nothing had. We had each other. We had our people. I was home with my pack.

Do dogs know places and the seasons? Do they understand the concept of change?

On my 15th birthday, Dr. Honnest, the vet, had stated that I was now a geriatric. That's his opinion, I thought then. I knew I was still a young, sprightly, "hot mama", at least in the moments when I was awake. But now, shortly after my sixteenth birthday, I am fading into my final rest, the rainbow bridge beckoning, the gentle tinkle of human tears interspersed with sobs wanting me to stay, but ushering me forward. I heard Victoria on her phone, "Mummy. I love Cloud and want her to stay, but I don't want to see her suffer." I felt a tiny prick in my paw, closed my eyes and stepped onto the rainbow bridge, scanning the life I was leaving behind.

Is there really a Rainbow Bridge for our departed pets? Or is it a human invention to bring us comfort in our bereavement? I don't know. But I like to think there is, and that loving arms, or paws, were at the other side to welcome Cloud.

20

AFTER THE ECSTASY... THE TOILET

Horse draw well when 'im memba corn.

Over three days, I had been immersed in a sea of consciousness, bathed in a soothing sea of grace at the "I Can Do It" Conference in Toronto in the spring of 2011. I swam with luminaries such as Louise Hay, Gregg Braden, Marianne Williamson, Cheryl Richardson and Bruce Lipton. I frolicked and played with three thousand fellow seekers on the road to enlightenment. What a feast! What a celebration of life! My life would never be the same, of that I was sure. The morning after, I awoke to greet the first

AFTER THE ECSTASY... THE TOILET

day of the rest of my beautiful, ecstatic and amazing life. I meditated, journaled and did yoga as I had promised myself to do every day from henceforth. Then I went downstairs and ...

My son had not taken out the garbage.

My daughter had not washed the dishes.

The kitchen floor was a mess.

The bathrooms were yucky.

There were clothes all over the living room.

The dogs had blessed the floor.

Now, high on my list of things I least like to do is cleaning the house. I love when my house is clean — I just don't like to do it. But I felt this urging, perhaps whispered in my ear by my mom's guiding spirit and recalled her saying "Cleanliness is next to Godliness," as she exhorted, pleaded and threatened my sister and me to clean our rooms. And I started to clean. The last room was the bathroom. As I knelt and scrubbed the bathtub I heard myself grumbling. And I stopped. Because I also heard the voice of the last speaker at the conference, Bruce Lipton, reminding me of the importance of PRACTICE in making the honeymoon last. I switched into a state of grace and gave thanks for having a house to clean, the wherewithal to afford this house, a bathtub, the time on Monday morning available to clean it. I even burst into my favourite songs from my ITunes Happiness Playlist: "I'm so glad, I feel so good, every little thing in my life is well," followed by "Oh, what a beautiful morning," from the Broadway musical Oklahoma, as I disinfected, brushed and wiped the toilet.

As I belted out Bob Marley's "Three Little Birds" in those beautiful Monday moments of cleaning the toilet, I wondered about the disconnect between what we are saying and what we are practicing. Are we praising the grace of Spirit, but complaining about our jobs, spouses, children, homes, bodies, and so on? Are we groaning that it's Monday instead of being thankful that we have jobs to go to? Are we beating up on ourselves for all the food we ate on the weekend instead of being thankful for the grace that provided such a feast? Are we complaining about our children not doing the dishes instead of being thankful for them being in our lives?

It is these "little moments of grace" that bring our lives into alignment with our higher purpose and open us to our higher good. Yes, the conference

AFTER THE ECSTASY . . . THE TOILET

and all the speakers were wonderful. Yes, I bought the books. But what will make the difference is my moment by moment practice; my moment by moment shift from fear to love; my moment by moment recognition of just how blessed I am, even and especially when I clean the toilet.

21

BUG MEDITATION

Nuh rain, nuh rainbow.

It's the type of morning that people in Jamaica don't believe exists in Canada, not even in August. Warm, even at just minutes before 7.00 a.m., it feels like 25° C. I stand at my doorway in my silk nightshift, the one I bought in India, my first cup of coffee for the day cuddled between my palms. The veneer of haze drifting past the light-blue sky signals that it's going to be a hot day. The leaves of the maple tree at my fence rustle, the metal and bamboo wind chimes above my doorway tinkle. A neighbour walks by dressed in a T-shirt, cargo shorts and sandals, his Belgian Shepherd prancing ahead. It's a perfect

BUG MEDITATION

morning to meditate in my garden. In a few weeks, I won't have the choice of sitting here. There's already an orange leaf or two on the ground.

I sink into the arms of the teak chair on the patio, draining the final few sips of coffee. I wish I had chosen a mug rather than the espresso cup. There is the noise of traffic on the street, the impatience of the drivers echoed in the sound of the motors. Too early to be in a rush, I think, happy that this morning I have nothing planned. Another neighbour and his wife approach. I hunker down hoping that they don't see me and stop to chat. The wife loves my garden and never misses an opportunity to tell me. Not today, not now, I plead under my breath. They seem oblivious to the beauty of the morning, and to the joy of their Golden Retriever that is immersed in its sniffing, tail wagging exploration, knowing that there is nothing more exciting than this walk, right now. They march past my fence, heads straight, eyes down, seeming not to notice me, perhaps upset that the dog doesn't care that it's the weekend and that one is supposed to sleep late on a Saturday morning. I would be too, except that my dogs are too old to clamour for early morning walks. I envy my son,

Shane, still sleeping upstairs, unlikely to awaken until midmorning, as most young people do, and as I used to, before babies came along.

I straighten up, press "Start" on the timer on my watch, rest my palms in my lap and shut my eyes. *Gently*, advise the gurus. I bang them shut. Time to meditate.

I focus on my breathing:

Inhale: I breathe in love. Exhale: I breathe out peace.

I feel movement on my right elbow. I try to ignore the insect. It continues to scurry along my arm, as if there is some yummy morsel of food hidden there. Another insect, this one a little larger, crawls down my left shin. It's big enough to tickle. I want to laugh. No. What I really want to do is brush it away. Or kill it.

I breathe in love. I breathe out peace.

A third insect lands on my neck, certain that it will find breakfast in the dense forest that is my hair. It has brought its family to the feast, for now I feel all the brothers, sisters, cousins, children foraging. I can't take it anymore. Eyes still closed, I lash out at my arms, legs, head, neck. The stings of my slaps bring relief. The insects are gone, I celebrate. I rest

BUG MEDITATION

my hands in my lap and breathe. The insects return to continue their business of scrounging at the smorgasbord that is my body.

I am tempted to peep at my watch to see how many seconds are left in my 20-minute meditation. Seconds? 11:10 minutes the clock displays through the slits of my eyes. Should I pause the timer, go inside and continue the meditation there? What would the Buddha do? I visualise him on a mountain high in the Himalaya, snow swirling around him, but sitting still, oblivious to everything — the cold, the snow, the wind — or, on the banks of a tropical river like the Ganges, mosquitoes buzzing, crocodiles lurking in the water. But he sits still. I decide to stay on my patio. If the Buddha can, I will.

I breathe in love. I breathe out peace.

The scent of tobacco invades my nostrils. Without opening my eyes, I know this is the neighbour four doors down, who does a cigarette stroll at least twice per day. I often wonder if he works, or is he one of those new immigrants with a PhD who can't get a job in Canada? Perhaps he has wondered the same about me. He is meditative in his amble, slow, deliberate, inhaling the cigarette in unison with his steps. Does he too recite a mantra? *"I breathe in nicotine. I breathe out poison?"* Or some such thing? I have never smoked, so I can't know. Oxygen is my addiction.

I breathe from deep within my body and become as still as the Confucius statue in my garden. The insects continue their exploration of my body. My thesis is that if I sit still enough, they will get bored and leave. No such luck. My inert body is just as enticing. I notice that I am less bothered, so I resist the urge to brush and slap the insects away. I deepen my breathing, sounding like a truck labouring up a winding mountain road in Jamaica. The Buddha would not hurt or kill any sentient being, and neither shall I.

Feral thoughts interrupt the inhale/exhale rhythm. What if the insect is a mosquito or a wasp? I recall reading in a National Geographic magazine a few months ago that the mosquito is the deadliest creature on earth as it kills more humans than any other animal, including man. I was not surprised, having felt their spear-like sting numerous times, been bedridden with aching joints from dengue fever, and driven crazy by the thunderous zing of a single mosquito deep in my ear canal. The image of the

BUG MEDITATION

wasp nest that my sister discovered in her garden days prior, surfaces. Could I sit still in meditation if there was a wasp, or a hive of wasps haloing my head? Or a mosquito in my ear? What would the Buddha do?

I breathe in love. I breathe out peace.

My mother meditated every morning in her later years. She called it her quiet time. No-one dared disturb her. But I loved to watch her, seated in a chair on my patio, spine straight, hands that used to scratch my childhood back now nestled in her lap, eyelids gently closed, the epitome of peaceful abiding. Or so I thought: she would complain to me that she was frustrated at not being able stop the rush of thoughts. She consulted her meditation teacher, Rev. Elma, who told her to think of the thoughts as clouds, passing wisps in the sky. "Just watch them pass, Daisy," Rev. Elma told her. From then on, she would sit, spine erect even as she aged, and watch the clouds of her mind through closed eyes. I smile, a tiny tear or two of longing dusting my eyelashes. I return to stillness in body and mind.

I breathe in love. I breathe out peace.

Then, off I go again – what if a raccoon turns up?

I remember the twin teenagers in the tree against my fence a few weeks ago, heading home after a night of hard work rummaging garbage and being pests. They had peered with menace at Itsy, my little dog, and I had wondered then if raccoons are carnivorous. I grabbed the barking Itsy away as they crawled up the tree and disappeared to their diurnal home. But what if they came back now? Could I continue to sit still while they bored their beady eyes at me, seeking Itsy for breakfast? Or this being Canada, what if a bear turned up? Or a coyote? I once saw a coyote in the park two blocks from my home, so it's quite possible. What would the Buddha do?

I breathe in love. I breathe out peace.

The insects continue their exploration of my body. I watch the clouds of my mind pass. The timer sounds: 20 minutes are up.

"Already?" I wonder, as I rub my arm and feel a small bump where the first insect had been crawling. "That was quick."

WHERE MI NAVEL STRING BURY: MY JAMAICAN FOUNDATION

As my journey of joy weaves through hills and valleys, one constant is Jamaica, land of my birth and home of my heart. There is a tradition in Jamaica that when a baby is born, the navel string, i.e. the umbilical cord, is buried and a new tree planted, as a way to keep the person attached to his or her native land. You will often hear a Jamaican say that they are going "where mi navel string bury". They are going home.

I share a Jamaican proverb or lines from a folk song at the beginning of each chapter, a reminder from whence I came and the foundation of wherever I go. There is no standard spelling for Jamaican Patois, it being an oral language. Hence, I have utilised spelling that I hope bridges the flavour of the language and makes it meaningful to any reader.

I am very grateful to my dear friend and soul sister, Yvonne McCalla-Sobers, for assisting me with the appropriate and perfect proverbs, and their meanings. She was at pains to point out to me that: *Proverbs are part of folklore. They therefore cross boundaries of geography, and culture, although some may be unique to particular countries or regions. Jamaican proverbs, for example, generally owe their origins to Africa, Europe, and the Caribbean. A proverb such as "No rain, no rainbow" is known universally even if commonly used in Jamaica. On the other hand, "Tek bad someting mek laugh" describes a uniquely Jamaican trait of laughing to keep from crying.*

I: A BEAUTIFUL DYING:

Fi mi love have lion heart,
Strong and everlasting, only fi yuh. (Folk Song)

(Translation: I love you with the heart of a lion. My love is strong and everlasting, and it is for you only.)

This folk song is one of my favourites. It speaks to a love that endures beyond any challenge or circumstance; one that lasts forever.

2: I KEEP LOSING DIAMOND EARRINGS:

What a fi yu, cyaan be un fi yu.

(Translation: What is yours cannot cease to be yours.)

Despite the appearance of loss, I know that at a deeper level than the material, I cannot be separated from what is mine. It is a constant reminder to me to be happy and grateful for what I have, and not to mourn what I don't have.

3: THE MAIDEN AUNT:

What goat do, kid follow.

(Translation: The baby goat will do what the mother goat does.)

People will follow the example set by those they see as loving and protecting them, even though they might not be biological parents. We have many who mother and father us in our lives, and who blaze courageous paths for us to follow.

4: NO-ONE EVER WANTS THE BOTTOM BUNK:

Family stick wi bend but it won' bruk.

(Translation: The family is like a stick that is flexible enough to bend, but is too strong to break.)

A close-knit family will react to pressure, but not succumb to it. My family got closer and stronger as we widened our embrace, and this has continued to grow over the decades. Now, despite or maybe because, of the "bends," our love for each other is like "lion heart".

5: MY FATHER'S BOSS:

Every long lane 'ave a turnin'.

(Translation: No matter how long the lane may be, it will turn at some point.)

No matter how terrible a situation seems at the time, one thing I have come to know is that it will not last forever. Guaranteed!

6: A CHANCE ENCOUNTER WITH A PIPE:

Di deeper yuh dig, di richer di soil.

(Translation: The more deeply you dig, the richer the soil will be.)

What joy there is to find great value by being genuinely interested in the people I meet and probing beneath the obvious. This makes for rich relationships, even if only for fleeting moments.

7: CROWNING GLORY:

Who di cap fit, let dem wear it.

(Translation: Wear the cap if it fits you.)

The journey of accepting responsibility for what applies to me, including how I view myself, is a long and arduous one. But what joy to finally wear the cap that brings me joy!

8: THE ARTIST:

Di more yuh chop breadfruit root, di more it spring.

(Translation: Breadfruit roots will spring, the more often they are cut.)

The more I practice a skill is the more adept I become at that skill, despite criticism by others. Just keep practicing.

9: BUTTERFLY WINGS:

Time longer dan rope.

(Translation: Time is longer than a piece of rope.)

The journey of joy is a patient one. I am learning to be patient and watch my life unfold in the right and perfect time.

10: LAUGHING AT THE DIRTY DISHES:

Tek some, leave some.

(Translation: Take some and leave some.)

Everything does not have to be accomplished all at once, if at all. Another reminder to be patient.

11: HAPPINESS BACKLASH:

Belief kill an' belief cure.

(Translation: What you believe can kill and it can also cure.)

My beliefs determine whether I interpret my experiences as positive or negative, and those lenses determine the quality of my life.

12: SMASHED AND IMPERFECT THINGS:

Cotton tree fall down, ram goat jump ovah it.

(Translation: When a cotton tree falls, a goat is able to jump over it.)

Unfortunate happenings present opportunities that would not otherwise exist. There is good in everything. Look for it.

13: YOU DESERVE A NAME:

Good fren better dan pocket money.

(Translation: It is better to have a good friend than to have money in your pocket.)

Wealth cannot replace a friend who cares for me and looks out for my interest. I am blessed with so many good friends.

14: FROM HOME:

Learn fi dance a yard before yuh dance abroad.

(Translation: Learn to dance at home before you dance abroad.)

It's so important to make sure I practice my skills before I perform the skills in an unfamiliar place. Even if the "dance" is different, I can still dance.

15: THE DAY CAN WAIT:

Di only ting for me, is mi bowl a bwiling caffee in di mawnin. (Folk Song)

(Translation: The only thing for me is a steaming hot mug of coffee on mornings.)

Morning coffee is my passion, part of my ritual that gets my day off to a good start – no apologies!

16: MISS CHIN PICKS UP THE POOP:

Tek bad sinting mek laugh.

(Translation: Make a joke out of something that is not meant to be funny at all.)

Find humour in serious matters to lighten feelings and shift perceptions. Jamaicans, me included, are very good at this. It's what makes us so resilient.

17: TO HOME:

New broom sweep clean but ol' broom know di corner.

(Translation: A new broom sweeps clean, but an old broom knows where the corners are.)

Someone new to a situation may make lots of changes to show how efficient they are; but the person accustomed to the situation will be expert at knowing the less obvious complexities. I have learned to accept and love the "old brooms" in my life, even whilst welcoming the new ones.

18: BAY STREET TO BAYVIEW:

A pound ah fret cyaan pay an ounce ah debt.

(Translation: A pound of fretting about a situation cannot pay back an ounce of debt.)

Worry will not solve a problem. Easier said than done, but it is so true.

19: A CLOUD OF LOVE:

Every dog 'ave 'im day, an' every puss, 'im 4 o'clock.

(Translation: Every dog has his day, and every cat has his 4 o'clock.)

Everyone will succeed and feel special at some point in their lives. For my dogs, every day is their day.

20: AFTER THE ECSTASY . . . THE TOILET:

Horse draw well when 'im memba corn.

(Translation: A horse pulls a cart well when he

remembers there is corn for him/her when the task is done.)

The thought of a reward at the end makes it easier to complete a task that may seem arduous. But sometimes, the "corn" is about being joyful in the task.

21: BUG MEDITATION:

Nuh rain, nuh rainbow.

(Translation: Without the rain, there is no rainbow.)

For beauty, for good to appear in my life, I have to experience discomfort and sometimes pain, which makes me appreciate my good even more.

IN GRATITUDE:

There's a warm and cosy blanket of gratitude for everyone who has ever touched my life, for you have brought me to this place. In particular, a big "thanks" to those named and anonymous, about whom I have written, for providing me with situations upon which to reflect and learn. To the readers of my first book, *Free and Laughing: Spiritual Insights in EveryDay Moments*, and my blog: thank you for consistently asking "When are you publishing the next book?" and patiently waiting for it. And to the following angels who have helped me birth *Forget It! What's the Point?*

To Archbishop Tutu: thank you for the example you have set for living one's life with integrity and joy. I am deeply grateful to you for writing the Foreword.

To Carole Adriaans: for your constant encouragement and support, and for always remembering how much I love the dear Archbishop.

IN GRATITUDE

To my teachers at the University of Toronto School of Continuing Studies Creative Writing Program:

Ranjini George: this book would not have happened without you. You gently pushed, prodded, goaded, encouraged and supported me through the Certificate in Creative Writing and my Final Project, building my confidence as a writer. "Go deeper Marguerite," "We need to see the place," "I want to know more about this person." I have learned so much from you, not just about writing, but also about meditation, presence and grace.

Christy Ann Conlin, Alexandra Shimo, Russell Smith, Alexandra Leggatt, and my Final Project evaluators, Lee Gowan and Marina Nemat: thank you for your commitment to your craft, and your generosity in sharing your considerable talent with me.

To my coaches, Nick and Judi Hughes: your love, sage advice, patience and support over the last 8 years have been invaluable in helping me start and grow my business. You are like shepherds with a big "A" for Accountability, prodding and keeping me focused on my goals and dreams as well as the daily, weekly and monthly tasks necessary to achieve them. You have demonstrated what joyful coaches look like!

To my creative team:

Robert Harris: such a joy working with you again. You make the mechanics of design look so easy. I will hold you to your promise to work on the book after this and many others!

Denise Gooden and Michelle Neita: for your meticulous editing and very sensitive and helpful comments on the manuscript. You approached the task with caring and love.

Yvonne McCalla-Sobers: Ah my sister – so grateful for your wisdom and guidance in selecting the Jamaican proverbs (and for the yummy mango pies and our usual bounty of laughter in our meetings on your patio).

Donna Santos, my photographer, and Sigi Bloomberg, makeup artist: oh those photos!!! How in the world you managed to make me look so good is beyond me. You are both masters of your art. And we had so much fun doing the photo shoot!

To my family:

My siblings, Douglas and Carole: no matter how much I expand and grow as a writer, I know there are no words that express the depth of my gratitude for you. So, a simple "Thank you. I love you".

My parents, Douglas and Daisy: for providing the foundation for this joyous, wonderful life I am living.

My children, Marc, Victoria and Shane: for forcing me to examine myself in order to be a better mother and human being. You are my gifts to the world.

My beloved Douglass: what a treat to have you in my life! Thanks for your love, kindness and willingness to engage in Marguerite's next mad adventure.

And now I shall pay the gratitude forward: to all who distribute, purchase, share and read this book – may you be blessed by it. I am indeed grateful to you for your support.

Gratefully and joyfully
Marguerite

ABOUT THE AUTHOR

Author, blogger, speaker, coach and facilitator, Marguerite Orane believes everyone in the world has an innate capacity for joy. Her goal is to help them discover it.

Marguerite is the Founder and CEO of Free and Laughing Inc., a business dedicated to changing the way we live and work, so that we do so with joy. She coaches and facilitates CEOs and their leadership teams in realising the value that joy and happiness at work bring. Her experience as an entrepreneur, a Harvard MBA and her curiosity about the mysteries of the world, as well as her life repertoire of adventures in consulting, leadership, travel, parenting, marathon running, yoga, dance and drama have been the foundation of this work. She recently completed her Certificate in Creative Writing at the University of Toronto.

ABOUT THE AUTHOR

Marguerite is the author of *Free and Laughing: Spiritual Insights in Every Day Moments* in which she presented six principles – Be Present, Observe, Release, Accept, Trust and Love. In *Forget It! What's the Point?* she delves deeper into the practice, by sharing her stories of releasing, accepting "stuff" and claiming joy.

Marguerite considers herself blessed to have been born and spent most of her life in Jamaica, and to now exercise the freedom to choose to live in Toronto, Canada (for the weather of course).

Connect with Marguerite and be joyful with her at:

Instagram: marguerite.orane
Facebook: marguerite.orane
Twitter: @margueriteorane
Her blog: www.margueriteorane.com
Or email her at: marguerite@margueriteorane.com

Made in the USA
Columbia, SC
23 May 2023